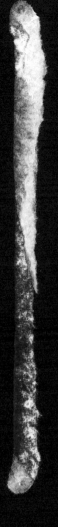

The MINI

Celebrating **50 YEARS** of a modern motoring icon.

CARLTON
BOOKS

For my father, who introduced me to fast Minis,
and my mother, who humoured both of us.

This updated edition published in 2009 by
Carlton Books Limited
20 Mortimer Street
London W1T 3JW

First published as The Mini: Forty Years of Fun, 1999.

10 9 8 7 6 5 4 3 2 1

Produced for Carlton Books by Essential Works
www.essentialworks.co.uk

A CIP catalogue record for this book is available from the British
Library.

ISBN 978-1-84732-373-6

Printed and bound in China

Contents

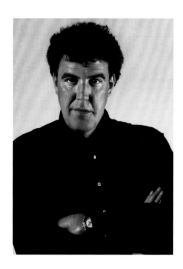

Foreword by Jeremy Clarkson

On 26 August 1999, designer Sir Alec Issigonis' remarkable design rolled out the party hats, made merry with the Hundreds and Thousands and rightly demanded large, wrapped gifts from all its friends for the fortieth time.

The fact that this little car has survived, more or less intact, the hopeless ministrations of Austin, Morris, BMC, British Leyland, Leyland Cars, BL, BL Cars, Austin Rover and Rover Group, in that order, is reason enough to roll out the bunting. And there's a strange sibling symmetry to the fact that, as part of the Rover Group, the Mini is now in BMW's hands; Sir Alec Issigonis was actually related to former BMW chairman Burnt Fishtrousers (Bernd Pischetsrieder), who has described it as 'the only loveable car on the road'.

It would be possible to write an entire encyclopaedia on the Mini, and over the years a great many people with beards and dirty fingernails have done just that. What you have here, however, is not an encyclopaedia on the Mini – although it has been written by a man with a beard.

Brian Laban is a very funny man, and although he may well have an encyclopaedic knowledge of the Mini, he'd never think to bore anyone with it. Oh no. This book is a funny and sometimes irreverent look at the Mini's life, from 1959 until today. It praises where praise is due, and damns when that's what is called for, too.

So enjoy.

Foreword by Frank Stephenson

The opportunity to recreate an icon comes along all too rarely for a designer. For a person who loves design, technology and anything with a streak of passion in it, working on the new MINI was a chance for me to unleash my creativity in a controlled and feasible manner.

The Mini was everything to anybody who had one – it was their first four wheels, it was part of their image, it was their friend and their love. Anyone who owned a Mini became emotionally attached to it. When 21st-century legislation threatened to kill off the most loved car of all time, a successor had to be created so that the legend could live on. But how do you follow an act like that?

In April 1995, BMW Group designers at studios around the world received the brief to begin designing what they imagined the new MINI might look like. At the end of the selection, my model was chosen as the one to go with. There was an obvious visible connection with its predecessor, call it DNA or genetics, while at the same time it made a 40-year leap into the future. Because the Mini had remained virtually unchanged since its conception in 1959, my strategy had been rather simple: to produce four designs showing what it would have looked like had there been a new model introduced every ten years, in 1969, 1979, 1989 and 1999. That final 1999 design was my starting point.

In my opinion it was important to project an evolution of the design, rather than a revolution. The car was already unique and bursting with character. Why fix what ain't broken? But while there's nothing like an original, there was room to make it a quicker, stronger, more reliable, safer, more comfortable version of its 'father'. It was ready to grow up – without forgetting its great heritage.

Since its Paris launch in October 2000, the MINI has received a very positive reaction from the public and press. It made it, it's out there and the demand for it is high. I feel extremely fortunate to have had the opportunity to contribute to its creation.

Introduction by Brian Laban

I know a bit about the history of the Mini. I was there: a genuine baby boomer. When the Mini was launched, in August 1959, I was growing up (though some would dispute the phrase) in Yorkshire. I had just turned eleven, and was a few days short of moving from junior school to grammar school. I was already keen on cars, but I distinctly remember seeing the brand new Mini in a showroom window and realising that here was something different.

I carried on growing up with Minis. We were a Morris kind of family. When I was just about walking it was a Morris Eight, then a very early Minor, split screen and side headlamps. Then (having forsaken an MG Magnette) a Cowley. And around 1964, a first family Mini, a red Austin 850 Super De Luxe, bought nearly new for a princely £335. Not my £335, not at fifteen years old. My father says I nagged him into it, but he was the one who started taking me to motor races when I was in short trousers, and he was the one who started modifying '480 NDT' the minute it left the garage.

Don't say you didn't.

And so it went on. A catalogue of ever more extreme Mini family motoring until the day I left home for London and university. In a Mini, obviously. I grew up with *Motoring News*, *Cars* and *Car Conversions*, books about Mini tuning, Weber carburettors and works racing Minis. Other kids knew the names of every player in the FA Cup Final. I knew the parts numbers of Mini cylinder heads and special camshafts. (Still do: C-AEA 731 was the one you wanted for a demon road car, C-AEA 648 was the really magic number for a full race engine, although if you talked fluent Mini, C-AEA 648 was called a 649.) We were at some sort of motor race most weekends, as well. So that first 850 had the treatment, and by the time it was a full-house 1100 with adjustable suspension, uprated brakes and big wheels, it would do the thick end of 100mph; and often did, between Yorkshire and the south. It also did several holiday trips to Cornwall, three up and every crevice filled with kit – surfboard included.

I passed my driving test in it, second time around. I failed the first time in a driving school A40. When I did the emergency stop, I was dimly aware of the back seat flying past my left ear into the back of the examiner's head. But that probably wasn't why I failed. He was safer next time round, in the Mini, with high-backed bucket seats, although I'm not sure what he made of a rather woofly exhaust and a tickover like a bad drum solo. Anyway, I passed, and that meant I started being a regular solo Mini driver.

I may have been a slightly wild one. Long before I had a driving licence I had a racing kart, but I only ever had slick tyres (I wasn't made of money) so I already knew all about oversteer. I learned about the famed Mini terminal understeer one night near home on a favourite ninety-left corner. A fast corner, but not so fast covered in farmyard slurry. Large-ish plough-on accident, larger bill, very large lesson.

Wonderfully versatile, the Mini has been put to many uses, most of which were very cool.

I learned other, more pleasant things in a Mini, too, being seventeen or eighteen by now, and realised that life wasn't all cars. No, go on, you know what I mean. . .

It was probably '480 NDT' that took us all from Yorkshire to Brands Hatch for the first Mini Festival in the late 1960s; and brought us quite a lot of the way back before the water pump disintegrated on the M1 just outside Grantham, in the dark, in the rain. But the good news came in the post a few days later, with second prize from a draw at the Festival in the form of what was then quite a lot of money, immediately recycled to British Leyland Special Tuning Department at Abingdon for even more speed.

There are still quite a lot of the tastier bits of that car in boxes at home, but the car itself gave way to a 1275GT, and that eventually became an Oselli-tuned 1293 with bucketfuls of power and an ability to get through front tyres almost as quickly as you could get them onto the rims. Nothing to do with me, of course. I had my own first Mini by then, a birthday present which saw me out of college, through the first 'oil crisis' and on to jobs as first a motor sport press officer, then a motoring writer.

Eventually, both my folks and I grew out of Minis, but we never fell out of love with them. Jobwise, I got to drive all sorts over the years, from road cars to racers, to rally cars, and even a Mini drag racer. Then for a very long time, ten years maybe, I didn't drive a Mini at all – in fact, I never so much as sat in one. Early in 1999 (on a circuit as it happens, but with a roadgoing new-generation Cooper) I picked up the threads again.

It was like stepping back in time. Everything was different but nothing had changed. It was like putting on a comfortable old jacket and everything came flooding back. Within a couple of laps the car felt as though it would do anything it was asked. But that was how it always was, and that was why the Mini was one of the greatest parts of growing up. Not just for me, but for millions of fans. That's why people love it, that's why it has survived to be fifty, that's why it's already a legend.

That was my story, this is the Mini's. . .

chapter one

One thing you couldn't deny about the **Mini** was that it was a small car, but it wasn't a small car like any other small car of its day. Or maybe any day. Whoever said that **small is beautiful** was not a small-car buyer in the 1950s. In 1950s motoring circles, small was very seldom beautiful.

size

what made the Mini necessary

8

August 1959: Alec Issigonis at the press launch of his finest creation, the Mini – the all-British people's car.

Rarely even plain. In fact, it would be fair to say that some of the most plug ugly and unpleasant small cars of all time gasped and wheezed their way onto the roads of Europe back then, their drivers perched in what might pass for either a goldfish bowl or a fighter plane cockpit. Often they sat in a light-blue haze of two-stroke smoke that some of these 'cars' were too slow even to run away from.

There were some excuses. World War II was still a recent memory and although the 1950s generally saw increasing prosperity, the decade started with austerity and ended with crisis in the Middle East. All three factors played their part in creating a short-lived popularity for the worst kind of small car, and eventually in shaping a much better idea, and one of the longest lasting of all motoring icons – the Mini. Of course, the Mini didn't arrive until the very end of the 1950s, and a lot of water would flow down the canal (of which more in a moment) before that came round.

War: What Is It Good For?

To put it all into perspective. The War (with a capital W) may have been over by the time the decade started, but the threat of war (with a small w) certainly wasn't. There were growing

(Previous Page) The start of something big. A 1959 Mini.

The 1959 Austin version of the Mini as intended, sliding windows, exposed hinges, simple sophistication.

tensions between the USA, the USSR and China. There were the problems of Korea and the division of Vietnam. The 1950s was the first decade of the Cold War and people lived under the constant shadow of the bomb. And it was still a time of major shortages.

All of which helped to shape the cars of the 1950s. Getting Britain back on the road hadn't been top of the wish-list for an incoming Socialist government in the late 1940s. Long after the war, most 'new' cars were really newly-built old cars. To buy one you had to have government permission and plenty of time. You had to be well off, too. A 1946-built family car typically cost

exactly double what an identical car had cost when the design was last built in 1939. Wartime taxes, long since removed from most goods, still applied to cars because the government thought there were already too many on the roads. In 1948 any 'luxury' car costing over £1,000 attracted double purchase tax (a staggering 66.6 per cent) to offset a new flat-rate road tax. But according to the same government any new cars that could be built shouldn't be on British roads anyway – they should be on boats, heading overseas to earn much-needed export income.

Manufacturers were obliged to export at least half of what they built, even when they weren't

The people's car German style, the Volkswagen Beetle, rear-engined, air-cooled, very different from the Mini.

building much at all. Mind you, British industry wasn't exactly bursting at the seams with go-getters. Famously, in 1945, a delegation of British motor industry 'experts' went to look at the VW Beetle project, which had started before all that unpleasantness bubbled over in 1939. Their report said, 'this car does not fulfil the technical requirements which must be expected from a motor car. Its performance and qualities have no attraction to the average buyer. It is too ugly and too noisy. Such a type of car can, if at all,

only be popular for two or three years at the most.' So while the Beetle staggered into obscurity, Britain forged ahead with masterpieces like the Ford Popular, the Hillman Minx and the Austin A30. Because, in this country, those were the sort of cars that were the forerunners of the Mini.

Then, for the fortunate few Brits who did acquire a car, there was the problem of running it. Rubber for tyres was still in short supply. 'Pool' petrol (which had about the same octane rating as a bottle of milk with gas blown through it) was still severely rationed. And we'd *won*! In the rest of Europe, Beetle notwithstanding, it was worse. In Italy, for instance, one Ferruccio Lamborghini was starting his motor industry career by converting redundant military vehicles into tractors. . .

So Suez

At least the start of the 1950s brought a new feeling of putting the past behind and looking ahead to something better. Young people weren't just young people any more, they were teenagers. They had a voice and increasingly they had money to spend. There were even things to spend it on. Petrol rationing officially ended in the UK in May 1950, although the downside was that it immediately brought record traffic jams. *The Eagle* comic was launched in the same year, making a big thing of looking into the future, and the BBC made its first cross-channel TV broadcast in 1950 too.

By the end of the opening year of the decade, though, there were the first rumblings of the political crisis that would eventually lead to the subject of this book.

The Mini may scream 'England', but its roots were far away, on opposite fringes of the eastern Mediterranean. The real story of the Mini starts in what is now Izmir, where the man who created it was born, and in Suez, where the events that shaped it unfolded.

In November 1950, King Farouk of Egypt demanded 'total and immediate' evacuation of British troops from the Suez Canal Zone, which

they had occupied since the end of World War II. Britain said no, the Zone was part of its Middle East defence system. What they didn't need to say, because King Farouk already knew it, was that the Canal was a lifeline that Britain (and not only Britain) could hardly live without. It was the only way for vital oil from the Arab oilfields to be shipped to Britain and Europe without having to go halfway round the world, past Africa and the Cape of Good Hope.

Oil power. The suppliers had the world by the barrels. In March 1951 Iran voted to control its own oil industry, which had been co-managed by British interests since 1909. By August the Brits were out of Iran altogether, although not without starting a dispute which dragged on through the following year. At the same time, tensions around Suez were getting worse. In November 1951 British troops moved in as Egypt declared a state of emergency. This happened to be the same month that, back home, rival car makers Austin and Morris began a merger, one which would create the world's fourth biggest car manufacturing company, behind the American giants Ford, Chrysler and General Motors.

In a lot of ways, Britain seemed to be on a roll. The Festival of Britain in 1951 was a celebration of a forward-looking, technological nation. It even had its great 'Dome of Discovery'. (See, there's nothing new.) But back then we did have real achievements to celebrate. In 1952 the all-British Comet began the era of the passenger jet. In 1953, nicely timed for the Coronation, Hilary and Tensing conquered the biggest symbol of them all, Everest, which led to Tensing's quote of the year: 'We done the bugger!' In 1954 Roger Bannister raised the Brit-power flag again with the first four-minute mile. And in 1955 we entered a new cultural age with the launch of ITV (in black and white, of course).

But there always seemed to be some sort of catch. The Comet was grounded by 1953 (due to a nasty tendency of the wings to fall off). A year later, teenagers had become Teddy Boys, and where America got Elvis Presley, we got Tommy Steele. For the most part we were still driving very ordinary cars. In 1953 there was a price war in the British motor industry, with the big manufacturers fighting hard for the customers who were filtering back to the market. These events gave Britain the cheapest four-cylinder car in the world, priced at only £390. Unfortunately, it was the sit-up-and-beg Ford Popular.

Ban The Bubble

Barely five years before the Mini, the cut-price alternatives were no more exciting either – cars like the two-door Austin A30 'Noddy' at £475, or the Standard 8 at £481. Petrol might have gone up by fivepence in January 1955, to a heady 4/6d a gallon, but these were hardly the cars to carry you headlong towards the next big thing, as Britain announced a £212 million four-year plan to create a network of new motorways.

Again though, the timing was looking bad. By the summer of 1954, British troops were withdrawing from Suez; by the middle of 1956 they were gone. Within a month, Colonel Nasser (president of the new Arab Republic of Egypt)

had seized control of the Canal. A month after that the 'Suez Conference' opened in London, putting together a plan for international control. But Colonel Nasser had a plan of his own, and in September he nationalized the Canal and cut the oil pipeline. British troops immediately started to return; by October 1956 the Suez War had started and the Canal was blocked.

It was still impassible by the beginning of 1957, and all Britain's oil was coming via the Cape of Good Hope. Petrol for the private motorist was rationed to between six- and ten-and-a-half gallons a month, depending on the size of car, which meant a limit of about 300 miles a month for the typical driver. *Autocar* magazine ran a feature on motor scooters as alternative transport. But there were nastier three- and four-wheeled alternatives, as Europe looked for ways to make its precious petrol go further.

As well as the shortage of petrol, Britain (and much of the rest of Europe) was still short of money. Post-war recovery had led inevitably to inflation, and in 1956 the British government had started a 'credit squeeze' to try to bring it under control. All the vital elements were suddenly falling into place and soon the monster was born. Across Europe, the 1950s became the era of the micro car and the bubble car. . .

As for real small cars, yes, there were some in Europe, even in Britain. There were cars like the classic Fiat 500, the Renault Dauphine, the long-running Citroën 2CV, the Austin A30 and Morris Minor. There was the magnificently ludicrous bonsai-styled Metropolitan and even the 'ugly and noisy' Beetle.

The Mini was exactly four feet high. Models under four foot five were hard to find, hence the artist's impression. But the car really could carry four pipe-smoking adults and enough luggage for a cruise. Honestly.

The Man From Izmir

The man from Izmir was Alexander Arnold Constantine Issigonis, later to become Sir Alec Issigonis, father of the Mini. He was born in November 1906, when Izmir was known as Smyrna. At the time, Smyrna was part of Turkey; at other times, depending on prevailing politics, it was a part of Greece. And 1906, as it happens, was the same year that Austin started building cars at Longbridge, where the Mini would be designed and first built, and where the original

Mini would be built until the final example rolled off the production lines there in October 2000.

It has been said that in later life Issigonis enjoyed making something out of nearly nothing partly because of the way he grew up, with what should have been a fairly straightforward life of luxury made a lot less comfortable by outside events. Alec's father, Constantine, was Greek by birth, and by all accounts a bit of a lad. His own father (Sir Alec's grandfather) had founded a marine engineering company in Smyrna, which became one of the largest in the eastern Mediterranean. Constantine, however, spent much of his life in England, originally as a student in his twenties, but staying on to enjoy the wilder side of life and to become a naturalized Briton. He didn't go back to Smyrna and the family business until he was in his thirties, and he was already 35 when he married Hulda, who was only nineteen. She was the daughter of a wealthy Bavarian who had done the proper Bavarian thing and built the brewery in Smyrna.

To bring the wheel full circle, the girl who became Alexander's mother also had family connections with future BMW boss Bernd Pischetsreider, the man who championed that next generation Mini at Rover, before he got the bullet. In 1996, the very, very pro-British Pischetsreider said, 'The Mini is the only loveable small car. The others are just like bars of soap'. It was a shame to see him go...

Being born in 1906 meant Alec was growing up in Smyrna through World War I, which created a bit of a problem because Turkey sided with Germany. So although his mother was German-born, his father's British nationality (and his refusal to allow his factory to work for the German navy) saw the family under house arrest and their property confiscated. The good news was that Smyrna didn't have too bad a war, and soon after it ended an Allied treaty of 1920 gave around 80 per cent of Turkey's Ottoman Empire lands, including the Aegean coastal area around Smyrna, to Greece, as war reparations. The bad news was that a resistance movement immediately sprang up in Turkey, and in August 1922, under Mustafa Kemal Ataturk, the Turks launched a major offensive against the Greeks in their former territory. It saw them advancing on Smyrna by early September and burning it to the ground within another couple of weeks. While Greece signed treaties, the Royal Navy evacuated British citizens, and that included the Issigonises.

It was a sad time for the family. They left their relatively comfortable life with no more than they could carry, and were taken to Malta. While they lived as refugees in a tented village, awaiting their next move, Alec's father became seriously ill. Once he was hospitalized, Alec and his mother carried on to England. In 1923 they arrived in London.

The plan was for Alec to go to art school. He had had little or no formal education, given his unsettled childhood, but like his father he had an obvious talent for drawing. Alec's own plan, however, was to become an engineer, and he headed for Battersea Polytechnic, while his mother went back to Malta, sadly just in time for the death of her husband, then to Smyrna to tie up the loose ends and sell what could still be sold. Finally she returned to Britain, to start again with her son and what they had saved.

Thereafter, she was one of the major influences in his life. Until Hulda died in 1972, the two of them never lived apart. But it was a mixed blessing. The two were without doubt very close, and Alec's mother was always totally supportive of his career moves. In the early days, she probably protected him from some of the problems of organizing his everyday affairs.

Not the first major accident involving a Mini, this is Supermac (centre) at the car's first Motor Show appearance.

On the other hand it may be that the relationship, and Alec's own feeling of responsibility for his mother as she grew older and more frail, stifled his social life. As a younger man, he did enjoy a social life – often taking summer holidays in Monte Carlo with a regular circle of friends, or winter holidays on the ski slopes.

As an engineer he may have been stubborn and arrogant; as a man he was seen by everyone who knew him as cultivated, highly intelligent,

unfailingly witty and charming. He loved company, and he certainly wasn't teetotal, famously loving the odd dry martini cocktail and (depending on how many he'd had) enjoying the nicknames Ginigonis or Pissigonis. He was popular with women and apparently happy in their company. He would play for hours with other people's children too, especially if they liked things that he loved, like model aeroplanes, boats and trains. When he retired, in 1971, from

Issigonis's first big success for BMC was the Morris Minor, another car full of innovation and original ideas.

what had by that stage become British Leyland, the retirement present that Issigonis requested, very appropriately, was the biggest available Meccano set.

But in the end, his life was spent almost entirely with his mother, and his social contacts were mainly with married friends. He never married and it may be that he never really had any serious relationships with women. That was just the way he was.

Issigonis was rather more focussed on other things. He left Battersea with a diploma rather than the intended degree, largely because he didn't get along with mathematics. He took a brief motoring tour of Europe with his mother; then Alec was launched into the working world.

Automobile engineering was where he wanted to be and in 1928 he got there. In his first job, he spent around five years collaborating on a design for a semi-automatic gearbox (with no clutch pedal, and apparently no market), then went as a draughtsman to Humber, where he began to work on independent suspensions – a novelty at the time for the British car industry. In 1936 he joined Morris, under the control of Leonard Lord – the man who would ultimately be the other key link in the Mini story.

Even when he was working for the most plodding of companies, Issigonis was never the archetypal old-school British motor engineer. He wasn't that stiflingly conservative. He was a free thinker – yes, he was both stubborn and arrogant, but only in that he didn't care much for collected opinions and that in the end he invariably did things his own way. Asked once whether the success of the Mini could be attributed to either his own experience as a motorist or to market research surveys, Issigonis responded drily, 'I never did believe in market research. . .'

A Minor Achievement

Alec Issigonis believed in learning through experience. While he was finding his feet in the industry, he started competing in motor sports – mainly in hillclimbs in the early 1930s and usually with sporty versions of the Austin Seven, including a supercharged Ulster. Of course, he modified his own cars, giving the Ulster

independent front suspension, for example. In the mid-1930s he built a single-seater racing car, which became famous as the Lightweight Special. He built it entirely by hand, using virtually no machine tools, with his friend George Dowson. Issigonis admitted later, 'It wasn't so much a design exercise as a means of teaching me to use my hands. George and I learned the hard way how to build something for ourselves from scratch.' Later, it became clear that the Lightweight Special project was almost a perfect little microcosm of what made Issigonis tick – the original thinking, the total involvement, the sketching and building process, all surfaced again with the Mini. We'll come back to the story of the Lightweight Special, but by the time it was built, in 1938, more important problems were looming.

During World War II Issigonis stayed with the motor industry, where his job was considered to be vital, and he worked on several experimental projects, including a lightweight Morris reconnaissance vehicle for the army, and a tiny amphibian with outboard motor and tiller steering. Like the Mini, it had small wheels at each corner; unlike the Mini (fortunately), the floor didn't leak. Before, during and immediately after the war, he developed an independent front suspension for MG. Then, in 1948, Morris launched a project that Issigonis had also started working on during the war, his first complete car. It was a huge success that should have made him more famous than it did, long before the Mini. In 1942 it was codenamed Mosquito; it became the Morris Minor.

It was another example of Issigonis defying convention – Britain's first 'modern' small car, and as imaginative in its day as the Mini would be a decade later. It started, like most Issigonis projects, as concept sketches, turned into detailed drawings and eventually into the metal via Alec's long-term collaborator Jack Daniels, who would also be chief draughtsman for the Mini. Issigonis thought first of a two-stroke flat-four engine, then a four-stroke flat-four, but finally settled for an off-the-shelf side-valve upright four. The Minor had a unit construction body, independent front suspension using torsion bars, and unusually small wheels for its day – fourteen inches instead of typically fifteen or sixteen. True to form, he designed it by eye, and near the end of the project, when he still wasn't convinced by the way the full-sized prototype looked, he had it chopped in half lengthwise, moved the two halves apart until it looked right, then had the four-inch gap filled in – giving the raised line on the centre of the Minor bonnet.

In another step towards the Mini, he would have liked to have given the Minor front-wheel drive, but when Morris merged with Austin in 1952, to form BMC, opportunities for innovation went out of the window and Issigonis went out of the door.

He spent some time at Alvis, designing a car that couldn't have been much more different from the Minor – a big, expensive, high-performance luxury car. He started by building a 3.5-litre overhead camshaft V8 engine, a complex, clutchless four-speed transmission and an all-new suspension system with hydraulically linked front and rear springing. That was designed by another of Issigonis's old friends, Alex Moulton – the man who would design the rubber suspension for the Mini and, later, Hydrolastic suspension.

Alvis never put the car into production – it would have cost them a fortune. Anyway, Issigonis was on the move again. In 1956, the year of the Suez War, he was approached by his old boss Sir Leonard Lord, now chairman of BMC. With the carrot of becoming the company's Chief Engineer, he returned to Longbridge and the Austin Design Office. With all the goings on in Suez, Sir Leonard wanted a small car. Needed a small car. But Sir Leonard hated – *really* hated – bubble cars. He wanted a proper small car, and he wanted it fast. In 1957 Lord bit the bullet, put all the other projects in progress on hold, and set Issigonis the task of creating a new small car, a real small car, as quickly as he possibly could. And so the man from Izmir started work on what would become the Mini.

Every cloud. The growing threat of petrol shortages in the 1950s was the trigger for the Mini's development.

'With its **tiny wheels** stuck right out on the four corners, it looks broad-shouldered, muscular and **sure-footed**. Any resemblance to any other automobile you ever saw is **purely coincidental**.'

Gordon Wilkins (in American magazine **Motor Trend**, 1959.

He had also been the first journalist to drive the VW Beetle)

chapter two

The **Mini** would not be like other cars. The project Issigonis would make certain of that. The project was given the code name **ADO15**, the ADO standing for Austin Design Office, and that was about as far as the official process went before **Issigonis** put pen to paper.

Style

what made the Mini different

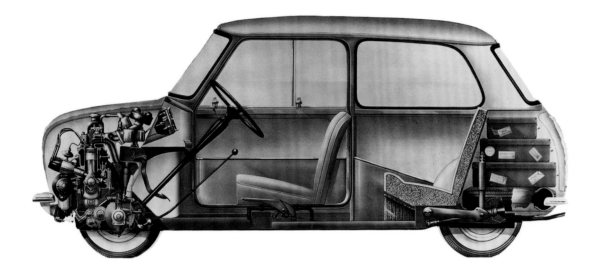

Maximum space in a minimum envelope. Transverse engine, gearbox in sump, and rubber suspension did the trick.

Sir Leonard Lord had actually brought Issigonis back to BMC to create a new, medium-sized family car, to replace the ageing Austin Cambridge. It was what he was working on when things started to go pear-shaped in Suez. It was what he was told to drop in order to concentrate fully on a response to the oil crisis. The firm decision to build the car was taken in March 1957, when Suez was still only open to very small boats and in the same month that Europe had created a 'Common Market'. Which Britain had stayed out of.

The brief from Lord for what would become the Mini was exactly that – very brief. Issigonis was to design a car smaller than the Minor, with maximum passenger space in the smallest possible vehicle. But it had to be passenger space for four full-sized people, and although it had to be super-compact, super-economical and super-affordable, this also had to be a 'real' car.

In 1957, managing director George Harriman told a pre-Motor Show press dinner that BMC was well aware that the public didn't want bubble cars but did want low-priced real cars – concluding, 'obviously if the Corporation can produce such a car which will sell more cheaply, they will do so.' As Issigonis related it years later, the gist of what Lord said at the start of ADO15 was, 'God damn these bloody awful bubble cars. We must drive them off the streets by designing a proper miniature car. . .' And that was Alec Issigonis' challenge.

(Previous Page) Advertising the Mini, 1960. Later the navigator would ride in the car, not on the bonnet.

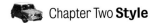

Take The A Road

There were only two other major stipulations. One, that Issigonis must use an engine that was already available from the existing BMC range. The other, that he must have the car ready for production within two years – which would be a tough call even now.

The time limit apparently didn't dismay Issigonis, nor did the engine requirement. In his own mind he had already further distanced the new project both from the bubble cars and from its smaller continental rivals, by rejecting the idea of a two-cylinder engine, and by sidestepping any thoughts of a two-stroke, in favour of a more conventional four-cylinder four-stroke engine. Such an engine was readily available in the form of one of BMC's staple power units, the faithful A-Series, which was well established in cars like the Minor and the A30. It was already destined for the A40, and used in Austin-Healey's little 'Frogeye' Sprite, launched in 1958. So Issigonis was off and running.

As with the Minor, one thing that made ADO15 special was that it would be very much a one-man car, rather than a committee project. Alec's car. Naturally it started to take shape like any Issigonis project, with a series of sketches. Many of them were drawn over long lunches and dinners, on scrap paper, on envelopes, or on menus. John Cooper remembers Alec Issigonis in later days drawing all over tablecloths, taking them away and saying 'stick them on the bill'. Along with two-cylinders and two-strokes, he had also rejected a rear engine. Years earlier he had experimented with a front-drive Minor, but at the time it hadn't fitted the corporate need and it was dropped. Now he went back to the front-drive layout, but he took the thinking far beyond that.

Small front-drive cars weren't new. The Citroën 2CV was well established, but even with a two-cylinder engine the packaging was nothing special. Issigonis looked at the minimum space necessary to seat four people comfortably and set a target in his own mind of an overall car size of ten feet long by four feet wide by four feet tall. He didn't need a conventional 'three-box' shape – he didn't like them – so an overhanging boot was not a consideration. He did have to have a bonnet; it just had to be as short as possible.

He had his engine: the A-Series. Conventionally mounted, along the length of the car (or 'north-south'), it would be way too long, and he'd still have to get power from the gearbox to the front wheels. It was logical to turn the engine sideways ('east-west'), but it was obviously more complicated than that. In itself, a transverse engine and front-wheel drive wouldn't have been new either. The German DKW Front had used the layout as long ago as the 1930s, and if you could count a single-cylinder motorbike engine as transverse, even nightmares like the three-wheeler Bond did it. But the DKW layout only worked because its engine was two cylinders and narrow enough to have a gearbox alongside it. Alec's four-cylinder engine filled the space between the wheels.

There was the option of putting the gearbox behind the four-cylinder engine, but that would have made the car too long again. Issigonis's stroke of genius (refining an idea he'd already sketched but not yet pursued) was to put the gearbox under the engine, or rather under the crankshaft, in what became an extended oil sump, with the final drive unit behind it. Or to be more accurate, that was one stroke of genius.

Another was the decision to use the smallest wheels ever seen on a proper car, just ten inches in diameter, which would mean finding someone to create tyres specifically for this car. In the first instance, that turned out to be Dunlop. The small wheels could be mounted at the extreme corners of the car and they wouldn't intrude into passenger or luggage space, but they did bring the problems of finding space for adequate brakes, plus the threat of excessive tyre wear, because they would be going round a lot quicker than conventionally sized wheels. To Issigonis, these weren't big problems – and as millions of subsequent Minis proved, they never really were.

A compact suspension, and driveshafts with enough flexibility to cope with fairly big changes of horizontal angle, even while the wheels were steering, were more challenging. Again, Alec threw convention out of the window. On the Lightweight Special, he had used rubber for springs, and he had experimented with rubber springs on the Minor. Enter old friend Alex Moulton, who developed a system using rubber elements sandwiched between metal cones. In one swoop they gave a lightweight, compact suspension which had progressive springing (useful for a car like the Mini, where being fully loaded with four people and luggage could represent a big change in all-up weight from car plus driver only), a degree of natural damping which allowed simpler shock absorbers, and attractively low production costs. When it came to the driveshafts, Issigonis adopted and adapted a design invented in the 1920s (by Czech engineer Hans Rzeppa) for the outer joints, and a simpler flexible coupling for the inner end, by the final drive unit.

Ironmonger's Way

There were other touches that could only have worked with one man making the decisions. To keep tooling costs down, for example, and to save time, the bodies would be assembled with simple external seams rather than the usual invisible ones. But those, and external door hinges – also for simplicity – became part of the Mini's character. It's hard to call these touches styling features, because Issigonis refused to acknowledge that he 'styled' the Mini at all, in the accepted sense. In fact, he hated the word. On his eightieth birthday, in 1986, he made a famous remark regarding style. Somebody asked him if he thought of himself as an engineer, a scientist or an architect. 'An ironmonger,' was his verdict. Certainly not a stylist. To him, the shape of the Mini was dictated only by the desired packaging. One of his few concessions was a reflection of the old Minor story. With the Mini Issigonis apparently made the original body wider too, in this case by a couple of inches – again, just by instinct. The fact that the car still looks fresh only proves his point that fashion dates and logic doesn't.

There's only one area where the Mini didn't anticipate future trends – it isn't a hatchback.

GO
MODERN...
GO
'MINI-
TRAVELLING'

This is the Traveller
you <u>can</u> afford

Pile in!

There's room
for everything...
except the
kitchen sink!

As well as employing midgets the ad-men also employed magicians. The dog is the smallest in history. Or a rat.

Issigonis never even considered a hatchback. In another example of his stubbornly individual thinking, he didn't believe in luggage space. He later commented, 'if you put enough luggage space for four people in the Mini, then it ceases to be a Mini.'

Issigonis did believe in practicality, though, and by the time the Mini went into production it had plenty of that. The boot was small, but the boot lid was designed to drop down into an additional, occasional luggage platform, with a hinged number plate that would still be visible with the lid open. Inside the car (at least, the car as it was first produced), there was an almost unbelievable amount of stowage space – everywhere from the full-width dashboard shelf to under the rear seats, in the rear sides, and in the doors. Issigonis once joked that the door pockets on the Mini were designed to contain the ingredients, in exact proportion, for his favourite tipple, the perfect dry Martini cocktail. To him that was a 27:1 mixture – 27 bottles of gin and one of dry vermouth. There was an early press photograph that showed a front door pocket stuffed with nine gin bottles, and room for one more, so Sir Alec must have been counting the rear pockets as well.

It was important to Sir Leonard Lord and to Issigonis that their new car would give a decent performance – not an accusation you could throw at the typical bubble car. It was another sign of Britain catching up with the times. In the 1930s, when Adolf Hitler commissioned the original people's car, the Volkswagen, designer Porsche's brief was to make it powerful enough to climb big hills and to cruise reasonably quickly on the new roads that were also part of the great master plan, the autobahns. Hitler ordered hundreds of miles of autobahns to be built in the 1930s. In December 1958, Britain opened its first motorway, the Preston bypass. All eight miles of it. They called it 'the symbol of the opening of a new era of motor travel in the UK'. A month later, in January 1959, it was closed by frost damage, but you got the idea. . .

Orange Boxes

The first prototypes of the new small car were maybe faster than was originally intended, but the fastest thing about them was the way they had been developed. From receiving the formal go-ahead in March 1957, Issigonis and his team of no more than around six close collaborators had produced wooden mock-ups by July. Come October, most of the engineering drawings had

been developed from Alec's sketches, and in the same month the first of two hand-built prototypes first ran. They were Mini-shaped, but were disguised for testing with A30-type grilles grafted onto bonnets which opened all the way down to the front bumpers. The prototypes were nicknamed Orange Boxes, because they were painted mainly orange. Essentially they were Minis, but there were a number of changes still to come. The engine was turned around so that the inlet and exhaust plumbing was at the back instead of the front. The engine and suspension mountings were given more elaborate subframes, the gearchanges improved (although initially not by much), slightly wider wheels were specified, and a brake limiter was added to stop the rear brakes locking up.

The braking performance was good enough to dispel most of the worries about not being able to get real brakes into such small wheels, but the overall performance was a real problem. There was too much of it. The Orange Boxes were built with 948cc A-Series engines which produced about 37bhp and they gave the prototype a top speed of around 92mph, which the management thought was maybe more than the customer needed. By production time, reducing capacity to 848cc and the penalty of an extra gearset for the turned-around engine had reduced power to 34bhp and maximum speed to 72mph. The size of the drop surprised the engineers, but the management was happier.

The project was moving to full-ahead. In July 1958 Sir Leonard Lord drove one of the revised prototypes for no more than a few minutes and

(Left) Achtung Messerschmitt! This is a KR 200 from 1959, the year of the Mini's launch. It's a different kind of car. The 1955 BMW Isetta (Below) was typical of 'those bloody bubblecars' which Sir Leonard Lord hated so vehemently.

'Two wheels under an umbrella'. The front-drive Citroën 2CV was pretty crude, but it stayed true to its roots.

promptly ordered a move towards full production. Within twelve months. And he got almost exactly what he ordered.

With the specification nearing sign-off, eleven prototypes were built, the last half-dozen of them being thought of as pre-production cars. In April 1959, two 'production' Minis were hand-built on what would become the new Mini production line at Longbridge (Austin Minis were generally built at Longbridge, Morris Minis at Cowley) and in May the first ten cars were built on the new Morris line. By mid-June production was running

at around a hundred cars a week, to allow a car for most dealers by launch time.

That launch was planned for the first week in September, but was brought forward to the last week in August. 26 August 1959, to be precise. A day when motoring changed forever.

Just over a week before the Mini's launch, the press had been invited to drive the new car. Until then it had been a far better-kept secret than we're used to in these days of spy photographs and scoop preview drives. Even the first press driving exercise wasn't on public roads – it was at a closed test track at Chobham in Surrey, the military's Fighting Vehicle Research and Development Establishment. Right next to what's now the M3.

First Tests

There were longer-term tests on the cards, too. By the time the assembled scribes started testing the new car at Chobham, another writer, Ronald 'Steady' Barker, then of *Autocar*, and a colleague, had set off on an 8,000-mile trip around the Mediterranean. They actually covered 8,197 miles and reported the adventure over four issues of the magazine. Their best day's run was 506 miles (from Benghazi to Misurata) in nine and a half hours – giving them an average of over 53mph. Their fastest stint was 82 miles in 74 minutes, in Libya, at an average of almost 66mph. And the longest distance the duo managed in a 24-hour day was 662 miles, appropriately enough in Turkey.

Over the whole trip they used 228 gallons of not always very palatable petrol, for an average of almost exactly 36mpg, which considering the way they were pressing on, and the conditions on much of the route, was a pretty impressive achievement. On the first 3,320-mile stage, from London to Alexandria, while they were still settling the car in (and getting used to it, of course, because on the day they left, nobody outside BMC had so much as seen a Mini), their average peaked at more than 39mpg.

When they got back to the UK, the car was taken away by BMC and completely stripped down for examination of wear and tear – to the extent that even the paint was stripped off the wheels, and the body was checked for distortions and flexing. The whole car had stood the test remarkably well – especially considering that this was one of the very first models off the line. Occasional overheating problems and cooling water loss turned out to be nothing more serious than a faulty seal in the radiator cap, but unfortunately the overheating it had caused early on had damaged one piston, so the oil consumption was more than it might have been, at 2,200mpg. Very late on Barker and his colleague lost compression with one burned valve, partly due to the overheating, partly due to very bad fuel quality (which happened ironically, considering where else they'd been, very close to home, in France!). They also suffered a problem that would soon afflict many early Mini drivers – misfires caused by water around the ignition system, which was now at the front of the engine.

Another problem – the suspension's tendency to bottom out and cause damper mountings to break – had been cured on production models even before the *Autocar* Mini got back to London. And that was virtually all that went wrong on what even now would be an epic new-car test.

In another nice little touch from BMC, some eighty new Minis were eventually lent to senior members of the press for longer-term assessment. This arrangement involved a twelve-month loan, with the option to buy the car at the end of it – which quite a few journalists did. Only a cynic would suggest that BMC acquired a very cost-effective new test team...

Long before the first year was over, most journalists were convinced of the new car's promise. The first reports appeared on the day it was unveiled to the public, 26 August 1959. To a man, they were universally ecstatic about the Morris Mini-Minor and the Austin 7, as the two almost indistinguishable versions of the new car had been badged.

Go To Work In An Egg?

Country Life headlined its full-page introduction in Motoring Notes, 'A Small Car of Advanced Design'. 'These new models', they said, 'undoubtedly represent a completely new approach to the problems of designing utilitarian economy cars. In some respects (they) follow the lines previously laid down by the designers of Citroën, Fiat, Renault and Volkswagen, but the conception has been carried to much more logical lengths by the designer, Issigonis. . .' *The Motor's* assessment started, 'Characteristics which have often been thought utterly incompatible are combined amazingly well in the new 848cc Austin Seven'. *Country Life's* finished, 'Certainly the two BMC cars are an adequate answer to those who until now have felt that there was no British car capable of competing with certain models from abroad. This is no longer a defensible argument.'

To be fair, the 'certain models from abroad' weren't quite dead in the water yet. However, there was another, much-hated target that by 27 August 1959 might just as well have been.

Bubble cars and micro cars pre-dated the Suez crisis, of course, but it was Suez that gave them a brief new heyday. Among the first of the bubbles was the Italian Isetta, a model built by the same company that would later build the fearsome V8-engined Iso Grifo supercar. The Isetta was beautifully described by historian David Burgess Wise as 'a strange device like an Easter egg mounted on a roller skate, powered, if that is the appropriate word, by a rear-mounted 245cc engine with only one cylinder.'

The Isetta and the 198cc German Heinkel were the goldfish bowl school. In fact, as DBW also recounted, the two designs were so similar that their makers went to court over them. But the cars were successful. The four-wheeled Isetta, with its swing-up front door (to which were attached the steering wheel and steering column) was built under licence in France, Spain and Brazil, and most successfully of all by BMW in Germany. Even after Italian production stopped, in 1956, BMW continued to offer the Isetta with their own 250cc single-cylinder four-stroke engine well into the 1960s; and between 1957 and 1964 the BMW-engined Isetta was also built under licence in England.

The Heinkel Cabin Cruiser, introduced in 1955, was a three-wheeler with a single rear wheel, driven by a 174cc air-cooled single-cylinder four-stroke engine, which was just about potent enough to get the blob-shaped car out of its own way. In 1957 things got better (just) with a 198cc version with twin rear wheels; but the Heinkel was never as successful as the Isetta, and it went out of production in Germany in 1958.

Like the Isetta though, the Heinkel had quite a bit in common with a movie monster: just when

1951's Fiat 500 'Topolino' was the rear-engined forerunner of the Cinquecento, and had its own touch of genius.

Before the Mini came along, the Austin A30/A35 was BMC's smallest car. It was cute but not very clever.

you thought it was safe to go out on the road, back it came. Again, like the BMW Isetta, it was built in England, by Trojan of Croydon. Almost worse than Isetta going on to build the Grifo, Trojan went on to build Elva sports cars, then McLaren F5000 and CanAm racing cars, and finally their own short-lived Formula One car, the Trojan. Not the Heinkel.

Meanwhile, back to the bubble car plot. The aircraft cockpit school of thought was typified by the Messerschmitt, and that had even more bizarre origins. After the war, an ex-Luftwaffe pilot, Fritz Fend, started building three-wheeled invalid cars in Bavaria. At first they were hand-propelled, then he gave them an engine (if you can call 38cc an engine) and in 1948 he created an 'able-bodied' version, an open single-seater which was powered by a 98cc two-stroke Sachs engine. He called it the Fend Flitzer, and if nothing else the name showed that Fritz retained a sense of humour, because 'Flitzen' means rushing past, or dashing along.

He followed that with a tandem two-seater, then an enclosed single-seater. And just to underline that these genuinely were strange times, these models were so successful that by 1952 Fritz needed a production partner, which he found in the form of former aircraft maker Messerschmitt. In 1953, Messerschmitt, the erstwhile scourge of the RAF, added the remodelled three-wheeler Flitzer to their post-war speciality of sewing machines, and called it the KR175. It was powered by a 173cc Sachs two-stroke engine and it had handlebar steering and two seats. It didn't have a reverse gear; if you wanted to go backwards, you had to stop the engine and start it again the 'wrong' way. The KR stood for Kabinenroller, which means 'cabin scooter'. And that probably tells you all you need to know. . .

Except that the KR grew up into the 191cc KR200 (with a reverse gear) and then into the Tiger, which had four wheels and 425cc. To be fair, it did have quite astonishing performance for what still looked like a long-wheelbase Dalek. Its two big problems were that its tandem seating wasn't as popular as the goldfish bowls' side-by-side jobs, and that it was introduced in 1958, just a year before you-know-what came along.

There was another British contender that, ironically, had its origins in Egypt. The Frisky was more minicar (a very different animal from the Mini car) and was designed by a British engineer for the Cairo Motor Company. When Britain and Egypt fell out over Suez, the designer (Raymond Flower) brought the project back to the UK and sold it to the Meadows engineering company, just down the road from BMC, in Wolverhampton. The Frisky was a four-wheeler (although the rear wheels were close enough together to make it look like a three-wheeler) powered by that old-English favourite, the 249cc Villiers two-stroke motorbike engine. The prototype had a Michelotti-styled body with gullwing doors, but it was no sports car. In fact, it was probably stretching the trades descriptions act even to call the glassfibre-bodied production model Frisky. . .

Baby, I Love (Only) You

Astonishingly, even those models weren't quite the bottom of the late 1950s motoring barrel. At the risk of offending any remaining non-institutionalized enthusiasts, there are a few more contemporaneous gems that we can't pass by. For example, the three-wheeled, glassfibre-bodied, motorcycle-engined Bonds and Berkeleys (including the ones that you had to kick-start from under the long but embarrassingly empty bonnet). Then there was the amazing German Brütsch Mopetta of 1957, (a 49cc single-seat three-wheeler which, at 5ft 7in long and 134lb, was possibly the smallest car ever built). And what of the monumentally ugly, Spanish, David three-wheeler; the fearsomely wacky, plywood-bodied German Fuldamobil; the 100cc, bicycle-wheeled French Mochet; the. . . Well, OK, maybe we *can* pass them by.

As for the more conventional opposition, even that was about to feel the effect of the Mini. When the Mini was launched, it added one more option to Europe's catalogue of compact, economical 'real' cars. Looking back from a late 1990s perspective, when there's precious little real engineering variety wherever you look (partly due to the Mini's own influence), 1959 was a far more interesting world. The pioneering people's car, the Beetle, was rear-engined, four-cylindered and air-cooled. The Fiat 500 was rear-engined, two-cylindered and air-cooled. The Renault Dauphine was rear-engined, four-cylindered, water-cooled. Citroën's 2CV was front-engined, twin-cylindered, air-cooled, and front-drive. Brits like the Morris Minor and A40 were front-engined, four-cylindered, water-cooled and rear-drive. The sporty Saab 93 was front-engined, three-cylindered, front-drive – and it was a two-stroke. The first DAF, launched in the same year as the Mini, was driven by rubber bands. In 1959, somebody, somewhere, made every possible variation of engine type, chassis layout and drive type.

For the most part, keeping the engine and the driven wheels at the same end was a satisfactory way of packaging neatly and building cheaply. Especially if the action was at the back, where the wheels didn't have to steer as well. That was how Dr Porsche packaged the Beetle to be affordable but capable of respectable performance and reasonable accommodation. A flat-four engine gave the Beetle enough power even for the country which invented the autobahn; air-cooling saved the weight of a radiator and water, and it wouldn't freeze in the winter or boil in the summer. By the late 1950s, the VW Beetle was strongly established everywhere. In the month the Mini was launched, August 1959, it passed three million total sales. And it was a big seller not only in Europe but, with 470 US dealers and 150,601 US sales in 1959, a success in America too: and that really did make it unique.

Just after the Mini was launched, the Beetle expanded from 1100 to 1200cc and to 34 characteristically noisy bhp. 34bhp was exactly what the Mini extracted from only 850cc. The VW had a top speed of 68mph, compared to the first Mini's 72mph, and it was roughly as close on acceleration. But a 1959 Beetle cost over £700 where a 1959 Mini cost less than £500 – approaching a fifty per cent difference!

Conquering The Normans

France's main cheap and cheerful Mini contemporaries were the already long-running Citroën 2CV and the slightly more exciting Renault Dauphine. The Deux Chevaux is another motoring legend, and in its way a real rival to the Mini, for popularity and individuality if not for engineering innovation – and just like the Mini it is famous for the way it totally transcended all class barriers. Launched in 1948, as a car for 'four people under an umbrella', it had a rather longer birth process than the Mini. It was first planned in 1936, when a French market survey suggested the need for a cheap and very basic small car.

The 1956 Metropolitan – shrink-to-fit American-style, Austin underpinnings, but still bigger than a Mini.

Citroën's suggestion was the 2CV, and they built 300 prototypes through 1938 and 1939. Like the Mini it boasted front-wheel drive, but in all other respects it was far less innovative, with two-cylinder air-cooled engines, simple canvas 'hammock' seats, and partly corrugated alloy bodywork that made early versions look as though they were built from old tin roofs. The 2CV stood for two horsepower, meaning two taxable horsepower: even the 375cc prototypes managed a few more real horsepower than that. Eight, to be precise. They were hardly sports cars, but then the brief had been a bit less ambitious than the Mini's: the French people's car had to carry four people and 50kg of luggage at 50kph. That's 31mph in real money. Even the Beetle could double that. . .

The war delayed development, but it was a recognizably similar 2CV that went into production afterwards – 375cc under the corrugated bonnet, canvas hammocks, roll-back canvas roof and all. Come to that, look at a 2CV today and whenever it was built it still looks like a 1930s car. Crude as it was, the 2CV was at least honest, and it stayed that way in some respects even when the Mini didn't, always offering an absolutely basic version while the marketing men increasingly piled their wares onto even the humblest Mini. So by 1959, the 2CV offered pretty much what it had always offered – not very much of anything exciting, but with its own brand of classless style.

Nicely illustrating the fickleness of human nature, the Dauphine, launched in 1956, was a more sophisticated car that never really pulled off the trick of crossing the image barrier. Like most of the other 'small' cars of the 1950s, bubble cars included, the Dauphine was rear-engined and rear-wheel drive – offering packaging and easy-assembly benefits without introducing the complications of having to steer the driven wheels as well.

All told, it wasn't such a bad little car. In Britain, the Dauphine sold well, helped by a television ad jingle (one of the first memorable ones on the recently launched ITV commercial channel) that went 'A penny-farthing a mile and you travel in style, the Renault Dauphine!' The Dauphine was actually quite cute-looking, and at least it had the 'real car' power and smoothness of four water-cooled cylinders. 845cc and 31bhp gave it a reasonable top speed of around 70mph (still marginally less than that of the first Minis). However, you didn't want to look too critically at the rest of the specification, which included a three-speed gearbox, and swing-arm rear suspension that was pretty good for comfort but nerve-testing if you were in a hurry.

That said, a Dauphine did win the Monte Carlo Rally outright in 1958. From the same year there were sporty versions from French tuner Gordini – the Dauphine equivalent of the Mini Cooper if you like – with 38bhp, a couple of miles per hour on the maximum speed, and 0-62mph reduced from a catatonic 35.7 seconds to a merely yawning 28.2. All in all, that still barely put the car on a par with the most basic of 1959 Minis. 'Compact' in the case of the Dauphine, however, meant almost exactly three feet longer than a Mini.

It's quite hard to imagine Lord Snowdon and Princess Margaret choosing a pair of 1957 Brütsch Mopettas.

The Mouse Trap

Fiat's Nuova 500 was an altogether smaller package. It was introduced in 1957 to replace the first generation of 500, the roots of which went back to 1936, and which was affectionately nicknamed the 'Topolino'. That's Italian for Little Mouse, and the original 1930s Cinquecento was described by Fiat as the world's smallest 'real' car, with a 569cc two-cylinder engine, a top speed of 53mph and seats and luggage space for two. It was built, incidentally, in the Fiat factory in Lingotto, the factory with the test track on the roof which thirty-odd years later had Minis racing around it, chased by the Italian police, in one of the most famous scenes from classic Sixties heist movie, *The Italian Job*.

With an update in 1948 as the 500B (with slightly more power but few visible changes) and a further update as the 500C, the Topolino took Fiat right through to the mid-1950s. The 'new 500' of 1957 was designed by the same man who designed the first – Dante Giacosa, a genius in his own right to rival Issigonis. And the Nuova 500 is still seen as a classic, one of the few truly small cars that really wasn't Mickey Mouse in the derogatory sense. One thing it can boast that

Proof that the Mini was always head of its rivals: a trailing Anglia, Ford's Mini competitor had a nice rear window.

virtually nothing else can is that it was actually smaller than the Mini, at only 117 inches long. Like the Mini, the Nuova 500 rises above conventional styling with a shape that almost created itself, and which still looks cute.

But good as the Nuova Cinquecento was (and it was good enough to sell more than three and a half million cars over the next 18 years), when 1959 came around it wasn't a genuine match for the Mini. Nominally it had four seats, but it had two doors and really it was a two-seater. Not surprisingly, with its rear-mounted twin-cylinder 479cc (later 500cc) engine and only 21bhp, it couldn't match the Mini for either performance or refinement. Although it could top 50mpg (which was as big a selling point for the Fiat as it was for any of its lesser rivals) the downside was that it would barely top 50mph, and at anything close to that the experience was a bit like riding in an overworked food-mixer.

Most remarkable of all (and this is something that speaks volumes about the Mini), for all its genuine four-seat space, for all its four-cylinder power, performance and relative refinement, the Mini was only three inches longer than the Nuova 500...

England Expects

The home-grown opposition simply wasn't in the same league. The next smallest car in the Austin range, the A35, looked like a toy, yet it was still, astonishingly, almost a foot and a half longer than the new Mini. Alongside the Mini, even Issigonis's Minor, a car which had a deserved reputation for comfort, handling and practicality, and which would survive well into the 1970s, was suddenly old-hat. So was the ostensibly new-wave Austin A40, styled by Pininfarina and launched less than a year before the Mini. Like the A35 and the Minor, it had a bigger engine than the Mini, in this case at 948cc, but early versions had the same 34bhp, and took 36 seconds to reach 60mph. The rear suspension used cart springs. In 1959, at £639 it was almost thirty per cent more expensive than a Mini. In comparison, the A40 suddenly looked very ordinary, with its conventional, conservative front-engine, rear-drive layout and its square rigged shape. If nothing else, it proved that Issigonis certainly had it right when he talked about styling. Looking at a Pininfarina A40 now, it appears laughably crude and dated. Now look at a Mini. Yes?

The undisputed champion of the quirky lookers, mind you, had to be the amazing Metropolitan, a car which wasn't quite a direct rival for the Mini, but was an alternative for the fashion conscious, the adventurous and the sporty. It looked like a scaled down version of a 1950s Packard, although it hadn't scaled down particularly well. The Metropolitan had a split personality. It was originally made by Austin for the American company Nash, as a super-compact runabout for the American market. Austin brought it to Britain in two two-door two-seater guises, drophead or hardtop. They were both strange, but both strangely appealing. The only minor snag was that the Metropolitan wasn't even as sporty as it looked. Under all the American warpaint, in effect, was any old Austin of the 1950s. Four cylinders (no scaled down V8 to go with the scaled down styling), 1489cc and 51bhp only overcame the substantial weight and barn-door aerodynamics to the tune of 74mph (about the same as the 848cc Mini). And yet again, for all that the Metropolitan always makes you think 'tiny', it was nearly two and a half feet longer than the Mini.

Outside of BMC in the UK, Ford produced the biggest Mini rival, in the shape of the new 105E Anglia. The 105E replaced the older sit-up-and-beg Anglia in 1959 and was the first really 'modern' small Ford, with overhead-valve engine and an excellent four-speed gearbox. It was immediately recognizable by its reverse-sloping rear window, but otherwise it was essentially conventional – although alongside the new Mini, most things were. The 105E had one advantage over the young pretender: it was the only one of the 1959 crop that was markedly faster than the Mini, with a very nice 997cc 41bhp engine, a maximum speed of around 75mph and very decent acceleration. Being a Ford, it was also a 'safe' choice for a still not very adventurous small car market, and it sold like hotcakes while the Mini struggled to take off. Oh, and of course it was longer – by almost three feet. But it was also quite a lot more expensive, at £589 (a Minor cost £590) to the basic Mini's £497.

You could also include the £702 Triumph Herald in the Mini rivals list, as one of the more imaginative alternatives. It was a throwback in that it still had a separate chassis (post-Minor, almost everyone else had gone unit-construction) but it did have all-independent suspension and it was quite sporty. If you liked that sort of thing. Amazingly, if you wanted a mainstream British badge in 1959, that was just about your lot. At the time, neither of the other two major groups, Rootes or Vauxhall, had a really small car.

How Low Can You Go?

You have to keep coming back to that word 'small'. To put the Mini's packaging achievement finally into perspective, consider this. Everything mentioned above, with the honourable exception of the Nuova 500, was nowhere near as small as you thought it was when you stuck it alongside the Mini. The Mini was ten feet long. Exactly ten feet.

Even the 500 was barely three inches shorter, and had nothing remotely like the Mini's interior space. As for the 'small' cars that followed, well,

let's have a look. The first Ford Fiesta (which was introduced in the 1970s in response to another decade's oil crisis) was more than twenty inches longer (more than 22 inches longer with bumper overriders). The first iteration of the sub-Fiesta Ford, the horizontally challenged Ka, was exactly the same – 11 feet 10.5 inches, bumper to bumper. And the minis from Japan and Korea, they were small, too, weren't they? OK. Well, maybe not as small as you think: the Daewoo Matiz – 17.6 inches longer. The Nissan Micra? A giant, at 25.5 inches longer. Even the super compact Daihatsu Cuore gave away more than ten inches to the classic Mini.

So, the corresponding generation Fiat 500, the Cinquecento? Sorry, seven inches longer. And the greatest re-invention of the motor car since the Mini, the first generation of the clever but controversial Mercedes-Benz A-Class, Mercedes' breakthrough into the small car market? 3,575mm, 140.75 inches, 11 feet eight and three-quarter inches.

In fact while all these 'small' newcomers were emerging onto the world car stage at the end of the 1990s, there was still only one car on the British market that matched the 10-foot compactness of the 1959 Mini – and in 1999 it was the 1999 Mini. Forty years on, size did still matter. . .

If you haven't got it, flaunt it. Brilliant Mini minimalism revealed at the Earls Court Motor Show, 1960.

'The Mini has stood the test of time because it was so new when it came out and didn't rely on any gimmicks. It has always been strongly associated with the right people and places.'

Paul Smith (for The Design Museum's 40 Years of a Design Icon exhibition, 1999.

He also drives his own highly individual Mini)

chapter three

It might have taken a **genius** to create the **Mini**, but it took a Goon to help it on its way – which says an awful lot about the **British psyche** in the 1950s.

class

what made the Mini socially acceptable

The Mini was almost undoubtedly the most significant mass production car of the second half of the twentieth century. Its brilliant design opened the floodgates for subsequent generations of compact, transverse-engine front-drive cars. It proved that small, inexpensive cars as well as high-priced exotics can be world-class racing and rally champions and fantastic roadgoing performance cars – and that cleared the way for the hot-hatch as the new sports car, from the 1970s right through to the 21st century.

At the other end of the scale, the Mini (often when way past its first flush of youth) put literally millions of young and cash-strapped first-time motorists onto the road in a real car. It won just about every accolade a car can win, including, in 1995, *Autocar* magazine's award as Car of the Century (a century of the magazine, that is – the car still has a way to go). Not least, by the time it reached the end of the line, some five and a half million first generation Minis had been built, even before the new MINI arrived.

Upper, Lower Or Muddle?

For all of its fifty years of achievement, for all the rave reviews following the Mini's launch – enthusing about its groundbreaking design, brilliant packaging, excellent performance and generally world-leading practicality – for all the legend, the Mini was anything but an overnight success story. In fact the Mini was fortunate to see its second birthday, let alone its fiftieth. But as it turned out, its problems were much more about marketing and psychology, especially in terms of the English obsession with class, than they were about nuts and bolts. It would all be alright on the night.

It is true that in its early days, the Mini did have its mechanical problems, and some of them were fairly major. To a certain extent, if you were developing an all-new (not to say revolutionary) car in the 1950s in no time flat, there was always going to be an element of the first customer being the next test driver. And that's the way things turned out.

Some of the problems are infamous. The most infamous of all was that early Minis leaked. The car had gone through its final test programme during a particularly dry summer but it was launched into a typically wet autumn and winter. It became a running joke that you got a pair of wellingtons with every new Mini, and that it didn't take long before the inside of the car smelled like a wet dog. Water accumulated on the floor and soaked the thin carpets. When it didn't drain away, they grew nasty and mouldy.

For a long time, nobody could figure out how the water was getting in. Engineers, Issigonis included, spent endless hours driving Minis flat out through water splashes, with other engineers flat out in the passenger space to see where the problems were. Foam-filling the sills was a partial solution, but the real fault was ultimately trivial, and simple to cure: one joint where the floor panels of early production cars overlapped had been lapped the opposite way to the way it had been on the prototypes. Lapped the 'wrong' way, it was scooping water in. It was soon changed.

There was another water-related problem. The first prototype Minis had their transverse

(Previous Page) Peter Sellers delivers wife Britt Ekland's birthday present. Britt thinks it takes the cake.

You could take a Mini, even a works rally car, anywhere. The 1967 Acropolis winner, off-duty in France.

Half-timbered house and half-timbered 1961 Morris Mini Traveller – BMC's version of style in the Swinging Sixties.

engines mounted with carburettor and exhaust manifold at the front of the car. This created problems – the carburettor tended to ice up in cold weather. To solve the problem, the engine was turned around. That protected the carburettor at the expense of needing an extra gearset in the transmission – to avoid giving the Mini one forward and four reverse gears. However, it also put the distributor and spark plugs at what was now the front of the engine, and the ignition system didn't like water any more than the carpets did. So, early Minis tended to drown in the rain. A temporary solution was liberal doses of waterproofing spray; the permanent one was a splash shield between the grille and the vulnerable electrical bits.

Exhaust pipes on early Minis tended to fracture because they were taking too much of the load that should have been taken by the engine mounts. Wheels used to fracture because they were taking more of a load than had ever been planned, as enthusiastic drivers began to discover the joys of screaming down country lanes with the Mini on its door handles.

Early Minis weren't nearly as good in a straight line as they were around corners. The fundamental Issigonis bits were fine, but early Mini tyres had a tendency to pick up white lines and deflect the steering – a problem which Dunlop helped cure by softening the shoulders of their Mini rubber. Fortunately, they didn't wear out as quickly as people had feared. At least, not if you didn't drive like a total rock-ape.

Then there were the transmission problems. Oil could leak onto the clutch plate from the main crankshaft oil seal. Rally drivers used to finish stages by throwing handfuls of sand into the clutch housing, though that was never officially recommended as an everyday cure. Syncromesh was also weak on some gears, until an improved 'baulk-ring' syncromesh design was introduced in 1962. And there were the smaller problems: the rear quarter windows that wouldn't stay open and the early four-bladed cooling fans that sounded like an air-raid warning (cured by an increase first to six then sixteen blades by 1962). Then there was the tiny rubber water bypass hose between the cylinder head and block, whose replacement either meant virtually dismantling the engine or performing bizarre contortions with triple-jointed fingers and lots of washing-up liquid.

Give The People What They Want

The good or bad news, depending on your point of view, was that not too many people were victims of all these problems, because in the early days not many people were buying Minis. Admittedly the car wasn't on sale until the end of August, but in 1959 total production was just 19,749 cars. Even in its first full year, 1960, the Mini still only sold 116,677 examples.

And this raises a rather curious point. Hindsight says that one of the main reasons that the Mini didn't sell from the start was that it was underpriced. That, every bit as much as the fact that people are naturally frightened by anything different, was a problem.

Issigonis' philosophy (shared by Sir Leonard Lord) was that the Mini should genuinely be a 'people's car'. The plan was to produce an affordable real car – as a kick up the lightly smoking, raspberry blowing bottom for the despised bubble cars or, more charitably, as an ordinary man's alternative to a motorbike and sidecar, or life-threateningly dilapidated banger. Unfortunately, the people the Mini was primarily aimed at didn't quite see it that way. To them, the Mini was a sore-thumb way of saying, 'Look at us, we're poor and we're weird.'

In standard trim, it was priced at £497; even a 1959 Austin Seven 850 Super De Luxe only cost £537 6s 8d (and £158 16s 8d of that, or very nearly thirty per cent of the total purchase price, represented taxes). Even so, the Mini wasn't the cheapest 'real' car in Britain. That was the superannuated (but never very super) Ford Pop, at £419. The Mini did undercut pretty much everything else. When its big rival the Ford Anglia was launched, also in 1959, it cost £589 (and the only really oddball thing about it was the reverse-slope rear window). A Morris Minor 1000 at the time was £590, an Austin A40 cost £639, and the Triumph Herald (also new for 1959) was £702. The foreign opposition was typically even more expensive: a Fiat 600 was £649, a Beetle £702, and a Renault Dauphine £796. Even many of the reviled and under-achieving bubble cars were more expensive than the first Minis: at the 1958 Motor Show, where they had been the most popular thing since sliced bread (what was the most popular thing *before* sliced bread?), the Messerschmitt TG500 cost £654 and the German-built Isetta 600 was listed at £676. (In both cases your money only bought you two seats.) But still the British public didn't want the most highly praised car of the decade.

Even now, it isn't easy to say why. Maybe the Mini was tarred with the same weirdness brush as other oddball front-drive minicars. Maybe people didn't believe it would work. Maybe it was just its size.

Toff At The Top

The 1950s had seen most 'consumer durables', not only cars, getting 'bigger and better' – the two words sat so easily together. In the 1950s, before the fuel crisis at least, even when a car was fairly small the ad-men had a talent for making it look bigger than it was. To look at some 1950s ads, there must have been an entire casting agency somewhere who specialized in midget motorists.

There was another thing about those 1950s ads. Every woman flounced around in a ball gown, and every man had either a tuxedo or tweeds. You'd swear the only time anybody in Britain went out in a new car, however humble, it was either to a deb's ball or Ladies' Day at Royal Ascot. Cars were still inseparable from class – and the class generally wasn't working class. When the first Mini ads appeared, they emphasized low costs and running economy. Mobil ran a magazine ad after the 1959 Mobil Economy Run reporting a Mini's amazing win – an average of 61.87mpg for a thousand miles. But this didn't seem to be what the market wanted to hear. If people bought a new car, it had to be. . . classy.

It isn't easy to say precisely what made the Mini socially acceptable, but it's blindingly

Simplicity had gone out of the (wind-up) window by the time Rover rediscovered the Mini Cooper in the 1990s.

Lord Snowdon genuinely loved the Mini. On the right is either young Lord Linley or another advertising model.

obvious that it was connected to perceived class. So long as the Mini was a working-man's car, famous for carrying a working-man's price tag, the working man wouldn't touch it with a bargepole. Then the London smart set, the film stars, the aristocracy adopted the Mini as the perfect car about town, and everything changed.

Quite early on, Issigonis took HM the Queen for a ride in a Mini in Windsor Park. Although it probably wasn't really her kind of thing, her sister, Princess Margaret, and her brother-in-law, Margaret's husband Lord Snowdon, became famous Mini fans (Lord Snowdon later became a good friend of Sir Alec). Yet there's a lovely

People became very patriotic about their Mini. Oh, and the Union Jack was also a very fashionable logo.

contradiction in their relationship. Mini suspension guru Alex Moulton has said that Issigonis – the champion of the Mini for the working man – loved his new social contacts. 'I'd say he was very snobbish, and he was enormously pleased, he really was pleased, about anything to do with the royal connection. He loved the fact that Lord Snowdon "adopted" his car. He was very much moved to admire the establishment, to admire the monarchy. And the honours he received gave him great pleasure. . .'

You could certainly see that pleasure one particular day later in Issigonis' life. He was knighted on 27 August 1969, a decade and a day

after his great creation was unveiled to the public. And he arrived at Buckingham Palace in a Mini – an Austin Cooper.

Although John Cooper's own specialist subject was performance, he recognized the class aspect of the Mini too. 'Once the car was established, it didn't matter if you came out of Buckingham Palace in a Mini – that was your car. But if you came out in a Ford or something like that, that was the chauffeur's car. The Beatles had them, and Peter Sellers, even Steve McQueen. It was the car to have. It was fun, enjoyment. . .'

For all Issigonis' love of the aristocracy and monarchy, there was a certain irony in Lord

Snowdon's attitude to the Mini. Lord Snowdon really was a good friend to Issigonis. He invited him on holidays, and was often seen playing with the latest Mini. He got to try the rally cars, including the one that won the 1965 Monte Carlo Rally – albeit with Issigonis in the passenger seat showing him the ropes. But Lord Snowdon's love for the Mini, and what it undoubtedly did for the car's future, were based on a very simple premise. 'I don't belong to a class,' he said in the late 1990s. 'I never have. I had a Mini because it was fast, economical, and great fun. That was the main thing. We had different engines, and the one we put in at the end was incredibly fast – a lot faster than my Aston Martin. . .' It was all the sort of thing that turned the Mini tide.

The Stars' Car

There were a host of other famous Mini owners in the 1960s, the 1970s and beyond. The cars were every bit as popular with smart young women about town as with smart young men – one more false barrier that the Mini was helping to break down. In the Swinging Sixties the car became the ideal fashion accessory for the likes of Twiggy and Jean Shrimpton, perfect for pop stars from Lulu to Beatles John Lennon and George Harrison, actresses like Hayley Mills and Jenny Agutter. Princess Grace of Monaco regularly drove a Mini around the Principality, and Spike Milligan apparently once did an advertisement for British Leyland and waived the fee because the Mini brought out the patriotic side in him.

Actor Laurence Harvey's new Mini made the society pages in 1970. It combined performance with luxury and it was specified by him right down to his initials in gold on the coachlined doors. It was based on a 1275 Cooper S and built by famous Mini specialists Wood & Pickett. It had special Minilite wheels under extended wheelarches, darkened windows, a full-size Webasto sunroof and a magnificent respray. Inside it was totally rebuilt, with soft wool linings and carpets, Connolly leather on seats, doors and dashboard, electric windows, and a state-of-the-art 1970 in-car entertainment system including a Sony slot stereo, a German VHF radio and speakers everywhere. It was further enlivened by legendary Mini tuners Downton, to what they called their 'Touring' specification – but the man from Downton did say the exhaust was 'rather louder than we would normally like'. No point being shy about a Mini that cost £3,500 in 1970 though, was there?

It wasn't as expensive as one that was built a few years earlier, in 1967 and, unusually, destined for America. That model was built by Harold Radford (Coachbuilders) Ltd – another of the great custom-Mini names – for Monkee Mike Nesmith. Again it was based on a 1275 S, and again it was Downton-tuned. The vehicle was made to Nesmith's own specifications, which included special seats, instruments, a radio and tape system, and a special ventilation system for warmer climes – including small vents let into the rear bodywork. It had metallic Sable paint and 'pink-champagne' upholstery. In July 1967 Nesmith's Radford Mini de Ville was

(Right) Sellers wasn't the only Goon to love the Mini. Spike Milligan was another patriotic fan.

Paul McCartney's was a fairly understated Mini Cooper S-based coachbuilders' car with the usual mods...

described as 'the most expensive Mini ever built', at £3,640. And that didn't include purchase tax because it was going abroad.

The most famous Mini fan of all, though, was probably Peter Sellers. This original Goon, comedy actor and highly popular personality about town surely deserves this title – not only for converting people to the Mini, but also for converting the Mini itself into something even more spectacular.

In his 1979 foreword to Rob Golding's excellent book, *Mini*, Sellers wrote, 'For thousands of us who had to get around London quickly, the arrival of the Mini was like the answer to a prayer'. It didn't take thousands like Sellers to put the Mini into a different social

... while fellow Beatle John Lennon's was similar except for the psychedelic, Magical Mystery Tour touches.

circle, just the odd one or two, and some high-profile publicity. He started with fairly ordinary cars, but the Sellers Minis soon became more outrageous, and were usually distinguished by trademark 'wickerwork' trim on their sides.

In 1963 he gave a Morris Mini-Cooper, with a detailed wish-list, to the well-known coachbuilders Hooper. What came back was widely described by the motoring magazines of the day as 'the ultimate Mini'. Inside, it was more Rolls Royce than Mini. It had fully shaped, deeply padded reclining front seats, with classic contrasting piping for the beige Connolly leather covering. The equally deep-contoured rear seats had a folding centre armrest containing a hidden vanity case. There was a full-width polished

Peter Sellers' distinctive wicker-trimmed Mini as film star, with Elke Sommer, in A Shot in the Dark.

mahogany dashboard with a full complement of instruments and an up-to-the-minute transistor radio, with twin speakers and an electric aerial – all very up-market for the early 1960s, whatever the car. The doors had matching wood cappings and leather trim panels and armrests, while there were electric wind-up windows where more humble Minis had sliding glass, string door pulls and bare oddment bins – although the rear bins were retained, fully trimmed, of course, and with folding lids. There was deep carpeting (it didn't get soggy and doggy any more), traditional woolcloth headlinings, and to add a suitably sporty touch, a wood-rimmed, three-spoke alloy steering wheel. It would be interesting to know

what the doggedly minimalist Issigonis thought of it all.

Outside, the 1963 Sellers Mini had 'Bentley-style' Lucas headlights, above two large front spot lights, plus new rear light clusters, and parking lights on the door pillars. It had additional bumper overriders, extended front and rear bumper mountings, and special wheel trims – though, oddly enough, not the already fashionable alloy wheels. The fuel filler cap was concealed in the boot, and everything that was chromed was re-chromed. It had special 'thiefproof' locks, twin horns, two-speed self-parking wipers and electric screen washer – and an uprated battery and charging system to power

The car was a birthday present. The 1965 birthday girl is Britt Ekland, in Radford's Hammersmith showroom.

Thirty years after it rolled off the production line, this Cooper S had a Broadspeed refit and said a little prayer.

In 1967, Radford built a Mini de Ville for Monkee Mike Nesmith, seen here worshipping its Downton engine.

all the new electrical accessories without killing the car. It had the imitation wicker trim, of course, which was actually painted on, by Hooper craftsman Geoff Francis – whom *The Motor* grandly described as 'the heraldic artist who has practised on royal coaches and other distinguished conveyances for many years on behalf of Hoopers.'

And that last bit handsomely sums up what it was about Minis like those owned by Peter Sellers and Lord Snowdon that appealed to the British class consciousness. Moreover, it is the key to what finally, and maybe ironically, made Minis OK for the masses who should have bought them in the first place.

Hoopers, with the sort of confidentiality they would extend to any of their Rolls Royce or Bentley coachbuilding customers, declined to release any details of the price of the Sellers Mini, but *Autocar* estimated it to be 'well over £1,000'. One of the other things that was adding to the Mini's growing popularity by this time was the opportunity to turn any Mini into an individual Mini, for a lot less than a film star's budget.

It was the start of a whole new industry, whose products ranged from the sublime to the ridiculous – and beyond. There were the good bits: bars to stop the engine rocking and struts to stop the exhaust pipe breaking and remote linkages to make the standard gearchange a little more positive than stirring a rice pudding. There were accelerator pedal modifications to stop your ankles seizing up on a long run, and long-range fuel tanks so you could actually do a long run. On top of these, there were all the sporty gizmos you could possibly want, from quick-release grille buttons and leather bonnet straps to racing-style fly-off handbrake kits and additional instruments. In fact, there were poor-man's versions of most of what appeared on the coachbuilt specials, stick-on wickerwork panels included, just like Peter Sellers'.

So from an almost terminally slow start, the Mini found its character, shrugged off the resistance, became classless, popular and successful. By 1961, annual sales had passed 150,000 cars a year; by 1969 they were over a quarter of a million a year. It passed the first million cumulative sales in 1965, the second million in 1969, and the third million in 1972. But by then, the Mini's production figures had already peaked. By the time production ended, in 2000, the classic Mini had finally sold close to five and a half million, but for many years towards the end, its sales had been cruising. The irony of it is that the more up-market its makers tried to make the Mini, the less appealing it became to the classless society. No class is classy. The pretence of class is simply tacky. Issigonis would have known that. British Leyland didn't seem to.

The ultimate upper-class Mini? A Broadspeed conversion to limousine status. Must have been for the Artist Formerly Known As Prince.

'I think the Mini is a design classic that has lasted such a long time because it is functional, economical, but above all pleasing to the eye.'

Kate Moss (for The Design Museum's 40 Years of a Design Icon exhibition, 1999)

chapter four

26 August 1959. **Mini Day**. Five decades ago, the world was a different place; **Britain** was a **different place**. There wasn't much else grabbing the home **headlines** that day.

Sex

how the Mini swung through the Swinging Sixties

GREAT
LITTLE CARS

MORRIS
MINI-MINORS

Great little cars. Great little pullers. Literally, it seems, if you're the passenger.

A report from the Earls Court Radio Show talked of many manufacturers switching to transistors rather than valves, and radios getting smaller and more economical than ever. Some makers said their sets would run off the same batteries for a year, and that transistors improved both tone and volume. You could buy a 'handbag sized' portable for just £23, and it only weighed seven pounds! The Mini was launched at £496.19s.2d for the basic model, a price which included £146.19s.2d in Purchase Tax – or around 22 times the cost of the radio. In 1999 a basic

Mini 1.3 cost £9,325, and you would have needed a wheelbarrow to carry £430-worth of pop-it-in-your-pocket radios. But if 'trannies' were a bit bigger and a lot more expensive back in 1959, relatively speaking, they were also the latest technology – so they were fashionable and they were the future.

When the Mini arrived, working on the theory that new and different was exciting and good, it should have been accepted far more quickly than it was. There was a real feeling in Britain at the end of the 1950s of looking to the

(Previous Page) Christine Keeler, Mini, more tea vicar?

future, maybe because the past was still a bit too close for comfort. Television was new enough to be exciting for many people, even in glorious black and white, with the choice limited to just the starched collar BBC or the newer, brasher jingle-playing ITV. Television could even make headlines of its own. On Mini Day, US President Eisenhower arrived in Berlin at the start of a European tour which would bring him to London a few days later. He met our Mr Macmillan at Downing Street and the telly showed the two of them sitting in their armchairs having what looked like a very matey chat, about world peace and, probably, the price of fish. It was a photo opportunity set up by the man they called 'Supermac'.

Never Had It So Good

It was Supermac who had replaced Sir Anthony Eden as prime minister in the wake of Suez, the event that had been the trigger for the Mini's creation. The Suez Crisis had ended as a bit of a fiasco for the Brits. At the end of 1956, when Eden was in charge, British troops had been obliged to pull out, leaving mopping up and future control to the United Nations. Britain withdrew because it couldn't afford to stay, and because America refused to bail us out. 'Ike' and his people didn't much like Eden, and even many Tories agreed that his government's handling of the Suez affair had been a complete Horlicks.

Supermac was our ray of sunshine. In November 1956, as Suez came to a head, Eden, suffering from severe strain, flew off to the Caribbean 'to rest'. In January 1957 he resigned,

and Harold stepped in. He was 62 years old, but to late 1950s British politics he was film star stuff. He saw his first task as to repair failing Anglo-US relations. He did a good job, and did it very quickly. By the time Eisenhower arrived, just after Mini Day, we were all good pals again. Macmillan was showing his PR skills. That televised armchair chat was his idea, and he skilfully steered the whole presentation – well aware that he was due to call an election soon. Which he won.

It was a new style of politicking for the UK, another sign of a 'modernizing' shift. The Mini was launched head-on into a Britain that had taken to heart Macmillan's famous spirit-lifting cry 'We've never had it so good' – first uttered at a Conservative Party rally (the political sort, not the Mini's kind) in Bradford in July 1957.

These were days of optimism and novelty, maybe the biggest feeling of progress for the good since the Industrial Revolution. The space age had started with Sputnik in September 1957. Technology and invention were never far from the headlines. In 1958 a Briton had invented the hovercraft. We hadn't backed building it yet, but that's another story. In 1958 'stereo' was the latest big thing, and before long every home in Britain had the soundtrack from *South Pacific*, while trains roared through tunnels, and tennis balls ping-ponged backwards and forwards across sitting rooms throughout the land. All through the magic of 12 inches of vinyl and two separate speakers.

In quick succession 1958 brought the hula hoop, the UK's first radar speed checks, parking meters, parking tickets, and anti-nuclear marches. Oh, happy days. It also brought that rash of bubble cars at the Earls Court Motor Show. At the time, even those were probably thought of as the latest thing in motoring chic. By some, anyway.

1959 was the year of the greatest optimism yet. In February the 'credit squeeze' officially ended, as the treasury dropped all borrowing controls. A few weeks later the budget slashed income tax and purchase tax. Soon after, the mortgage rate dropped to 5.5 per cent. In April, engineers were drilling test holes for a Channel Tunnel. Mind you, they'd been doing that since Victorian times. More realistically, the government had started talking about a huge road-building programme. With the Mini virtually ready for production, Sir Leonard Lord and BMC must have been feeling well pleased with their timing.

On the day the Mini was shown off to the press, 18 August, the proposed route of a forthcoming bit of M1 was rerouted to save an area of forest. Come November you could have taken your brand new Mini onto the first stretch of the brand new M1 that did open. In fine British 1950s style, the motorway attracted huge crowds of sightseers on its first weekend – they perched on bridges and picnicked near the road to watch the Ford Pops and Standard Eights scream by. In equally fine British tradition, a couple of weeks after it opened a group of five police chiefs branded its design as unsatisfactory. To be fair, the first fatal accident on the M1 occurred during the first week it was open.

That was the Britain that the Mini was born into in the final gasp of the 1950s. In reality, of course, the Mini became far more an icon of the 1960s. The Swinging Sixties.

Go Wild In The Countryman

The decade started with another classic Macmillan soundbite: 'The wind of change'. He actually said it was blowing through Africa, but the phrase was just as good a catchphrase for Sixties Britain as his 'never had it so good' had been for the Fifties.

The Swinging Sixties. The first decade proper of the Mini, and its most glorious. It would be the decade when anything seemed possible. Right at the beginning, that pillar of the establishment the BBC was asking for another channel. In February 1960, Princess Margaret (the Queen's younger sister, no less) showed just how wild and daring we'd all become, by announcing her engagement to a 'commoner', the photographer Mr Anthony Armstrong-Jones. In fact, as the son of Ronald Armstrong-Jones QC and the Countess of Rosse, he arguably wasn't as common as all that. As the Earl of Snowdon, however, he became one of the Mini's greatest fans and champions. And the lady wife drove one, too.

The Sixties was a decade of men venturing into space, of tension between the superpowers, of Vietnam, of the Cuban missile crisis, the building of the Berlin Wall and the death of John Kennedy. It was a decade when values changed, and the world relaxed a little, a decade of change, enthusiasm, boom and bust economy (at home,

It's a mid-1960s registration, but tiny details apart, the scene could be any time between 1959 and 2009.

In 1968 Cathy McGowan tore up her L plates and bought herself a Mini automatic Super de Luxe, for £672.

anyway), and of youth taking centre stage. In Britain, where not so long ago radio presenters had worn dinner jackets to read the news in syrupy establishment accents, regional and working-class talk became fashionable, on the back of new wave plays like *Saturday Night and Sunday Morning*, *Billy Liar*, and *Look Back in Anger*. The sexual revolution was on its way, too, and Britain was at the cutting edge. Early in 1959 a British Medical Association booklet on marriage was scrapped because it discussed whether chastity was old-fashioned. The Queen was pregnant, though, with the one who turned out to be Prince Andrew.

The Mini flowed with the tide. DH Lawrence's novel *Lady Chatterley's Lover* was tried for obscenity; it won its case, and the paperback edition sold out on its first day. The lover with the colourful language was the eponymous Lady C's gamekeeper, a country lad. It was a nice coincidence that the first variant of the Mini, launched in September 1960, was called the Countryman. Or the Traveller, depending on which badge it carried. Either way, it was that terribly British thing, the half-timbered estate car.

By 1961, Britain's last National Serviceman had been called up and with him one of the biggest downsides of being young disappeared. Another teenage worry was about to change forever. In January 'The Pill' went on sale in the UK; by December it would be available through the National Health Service. 'Children's Hour' was dropped from the telly in April and Gagarin was blasted into space (he came to London in July, and Mac called him 'a delightful fellow').

The Berlin Wall went up in August, and Britain started muttering about membership of the EEC – but nothing changed life like The Pill.

Sexual freedom was becoming a reality, a catalyst for losing inhibitions right, left and centre. Youth no longer lived in the shadow of the establishment; it burst into the sunshine. The Mini, meanwhile, showed worrying early signs of misjudged gentrification in 1961, with the launch of the Super that September, featuring fancy oil and water gauges and poncy ignition-key starting. It went even further in October with the Riley Elf and Wolseley Hornet, all dolled up with false radiator grilles, tacked on boots and tacky walnut dashboards. But in the same month, the first Cooper gave cause for hope. And the Mini was starting to be taken up by the fashion conscious.

Please Please Me

The Austin version went all modern in 1962, dropping the throwback 'Seven' name and coming out of the closet as plain Austin Mini. Well, not quite so plain come October, when the De Luxe and Super versions were replaced by the Super de Luxe. The MkII Elf and Hornet introduced their single carb version of the 998cc engine that would find its way into the Cooper come 1964. But in 1962, the Sixties were gathering pace. In February, the *Sunday Times* launched Britain's first newspaper colour supplement, with features on Pop Art, and Mary Quant – a fashion designer at the core of the new London scene.

It wasn't only clothes that were getting more daring. A stage revue called *Beyond the Fringe*

QUARTS OF ROOM . . . PINT-SIZE DIMENSIONS

The ghost of an idea: like Issigonis, the ad split the car down the middle and added a bit until it looked right.

launched a trend for taking the mickey out of well-deserving targets. A new magazine, *Private Eye*, did the same in print. *That Was The Week That Was* hit the BBC in November and ruffled even more establishment feathers. In the early 1960s, Britain was still laughably conservative. In July the first live transatlantic TV pictures were transmitted via Telstar. France sent the USA exciting shots of Yves Montand singing, which was bad enough. The UK sent a test card and 'greetings', which was Dullsville personified. Their respective greetings arrived in a country where 'Modern' art now meant people like

Andy Warhol and Roy Lichtenstein. Although Decca rejected a group called The Beatles early in 1962, the band topped a poll in the *Mersey Beat* newspaper. Before long they would be buying Minis with the best of them.

In 1962, the Mini became even cheaper than when it was launched. The April budget saw a ten per cent cut in car tax, bringing the price of a Mini down from £526.4s.9d to £495.19s.3d. It came down again in November, as purchase tax on cars was halved, but those moves followed economic uncertainty. Fears that lower taxes on household goods might lead to a hire purchase spending boom and more imports, plus a slump on the London Stock Exchange, led the government to try various ways of boosting the economy. Meanwhile, one of the Sixties' classic film icons, James Bond, débuted as a member of Her Majesty's Secret Service in *Dr No*. Like the Mini, oddly enough, the first Bond film had proved to be a slow starter, but soon people couldn't get enough of it.

1963 was a quiet year for the Mini, aside from the début of the 1071 Cooper S in June. However, it was an exciting year for thoroughly modern Britain. In January the BBC ended its ban on mentioning politics, royalty, religion and sex in comedy shows. So this drunken MP goes up to the Queen and the Archbishop of Canterbury and he says. . .

In February The Beatles recorded their first LP, *Please Please Me*, and made their national TV début on *Thank Your Lucky Stars*. The programme was the cutting edge of poptastic TV until *Ready Steady Go* was launched, featuring live music and Sixties icon presenter Cathy McGowan. It was the year of the Great Train Robbery, Kennedy's assassination, Jim Clark's first world championship, and the early rumblings of the Profumo affair. Guess which car Christine Keeler, the woman at the centre of the scandal, was often seen in?

The Mini was deeply trendy by 1964, when Britain was becoming fashion centre of the universe. Mary Quant had opened the UK's first 'boutique', in Chelsea, selling bold designs and short skirts that were 'absolutely 20th century'. Beatlemania followed the Fab Four to America and Australia, while the Rolling Stones offered a less winsome alternative to the Mop Tops. The 1275 and 970 Cooper Ss were new Mini alternatives to the 1071.

And youth culture kept right on growing. BBC2 went on air; so did pirate radio stations Caroline and Atlantic. The sexual revolution saw the opening of London's first clinic giving family planning advice to unmarried couples. But it wasn't all fun. Bank Holiday weekends in 1964 saw Mods and Rockers turning seaside towns like Clacton, Margate, Brighton and Bournemouth into battlegrounds. Topless dresses proved too daring even for London, though – three women who wore them were found guilty of indecency. The famous Windmill Theatre (where Mini fan Peter Sellers started his comedy career) closed – killed, ironically, by a permissive society which suddenly made its static nudes seem quaint.

Come Swing With Me

In October, Labour and Harold Wilson replaced the old Tory government as clouds gathered round a failing economy. The November budget raised tax by six per cent; sterling was sliding; Britain had taken over a billion pounds in overseas loans to prop things up. The country's economy was in the guano. On the bright side, in March 1965 Alec Issigonis drove the millionth Mini off the line, and May brought the Mini's first automatic gearbox option, June saw MBEs for The Beatles, and in July Ted Heath became Tory leader. OK, three out of four's not bad. . .

In November, two more signs of decadence appeared: a reclining seat option for Mini

1969 Cooper S with Margrave conversion by Wood & Pickett, throttle pedal extension by Paddy Hopkirk.

If you can remember the 1960s you probably weren't there. Mini enthusiast Twiggy, goats, strange days . . .

Flower power, psychedelia and the Mini were bedmates in the 1960s. People didn't do this with most cars.

Moke was rejected as a military workhorse, reborn as a fun car. This is a Potuguese-built 1984 Californian.

Coopers and new taxes on minis. The skirts that is, not the car: they'd grown so short that some were avoiding duty by pretending to be (tax exempt) children's clothes. Thank goodness there were still some guardians of decency left: Mary Whitehouse set up the National Viewers and Listeners Association to protect us from this downward spiral of permissiveness and profanity. Not sure what she drove. . .

1966 made it all official. In April, *Time* magazine ran the headline, 'London: the

Swinging City'. The story inside announced, 'In this century, every decade has its city. . . for the Sixties that city is London'. London – fashion capital of world, city of King's Road and Carnaby Street. You couldn't swing a fringed shoulder-bag for Kaftans and beads. British music ruled the world, with The Beatles, the Stones, The Who, The Kinks, The Small Faces and a nascent Pink Floyd providing a soundtrack for the decade. Try and think of any of them in the late Sixties without thinking of mile-wide lapels and

1967, student Juanite Neary, in a bikini, selling raffle tickets. Mini in a snowdrift. Answers on a postcard?

flares like wigwams. Or Union Jack Minis and suede mini skirts.

The new Labour government went with the mood. Our scientists were going down the Brain Drain to the USA, but pop stars, artists, models, photographers and designers were the new aristocracy. When England won the World Cup in 1966 we ruled the world, and Freddie Laker would take you round it on the cheap, maybe on your new Barclaycard, launched in June as the first British credit card. It would take your mind off a 70mph speed limit – and July's news of a wage and prices freeze, HP curbs, bank rate increases, runaway inflation and spiralling unemployment. On the darker side, pop culture was also pot culture for many, and acid-flavoured psychedelia was infiltrating the charts.

The Mini was still on the up. Production would be close to a quarter of a million cars in 1967 and it had won its third (or depending on how you look at it, fourth) Monte Carlo Rally. Famous people like Snowdon and Sellers were already driving it, and more were discovering it. In February, The Monkees came to Britain; in July, Monkee Mike Nesmith had 'the most expensive Mini ever built' (so far) shipped over to America.

The First Summer Of Love

It's often been said of the 1960s that if you can remember them you couldn't have been there. Among those who do claim to remember, 1967 is talked about as the year of years, *the* year of the decade of the century. It was the year of *Sergeant Pepper*, the Woburn Festival, the launch of

Radio 1 and the opening of The Beatles' Apple Boutique for 'London's swinging elite'. One film, *Blow Up* (made in 1966), whose central characters were mini-skirted models and a new aristo photographer, captured the essence of Swinging London – sex and drugs and rock and roll, hippies, Flower Power, Love and Peace, Hendrix. And the Mini.

The Mini was getting smarter. 1967 was the year of the MkII (or MkIII for the Elf and Hornet). MkII meant 'refinements': a bigger rear window, bigger grille, new badges and interior trim, better seats, bigger, squarer rear lights. The Cooper got an all-syncro gearbox (a year ahead of the others) and the Mini 1000 Super de Luxe saloon and estate were introduced; even the van and pick-up gained a 998cc option.

But while the Mini was heading north, some things were going south. The Stones were in trouble for being stoned, *Oz* magazine was in trouble for telling the truth, there were big attendances at the Legalize Pot rally in Hyde Park and Che Guevara (a Sixties counterculture icon to rival any) was dead. So was pirate radio – the Marine Broadcasting Act sending ex-pirate DJs, including John Peel and Tony Blackburn, scurrying to Radio 1.

More seriously, the Six Day War in the Middle East again underlined Europe's fear of oil shortages, and the UK economy went pear-shaped. In November 1967 the pound was devalued by 14.3 per cent. The credit squeeze was tightened again, bank rate and taxes were up: Britain was borrowing – big time. Wilson presented the moves as the key to economic expansion, and boom times by 1969: 'It does not mean, of course,' Wilson reassured the public, 'that the pound here in Britain, in your pocket or purse or in your bank has been devalued'. He had his fingers crossed when he said that, and not just for luck.

It did the Mini less harm than some. This was the kind of buckle-down adversity the car had been designed for. Sales kept growing, and every year, from 1968 to 1971, set new records. 1968, though, was a messy one. The March budget raised taxes again, along with petrol duty – the arrival of Britain's first decimal coins couldn't hide it. Youth culture was getting stroppy: there were anti-Vietnam demos and sit-ins in London and student riots in Paris. The older generation was no better: JFK's brother Bobby was assassinated, as was Dr Martin Luther King. Tanks rolled into Czechoslovakia, the Pope said no to birth control for Catholics, and BMC and Leyland announced merger plans.

Some bits kept swinging. The day after stage censorship was relaxed, the cast of *Hair*, the 'Tribal-Love-Rock-Musical', went naked. On the streets, the mini skirt was at its shortest – with cleaners advertising two (old) pence per inch to clean them. In the true spirit of the blitz, under a Union Jack banner just like many a Mini roof, the 'I'm Backing Britain' campaign was launched, by five typists in Surbiton.

Again, the Mini was moving onwards and upwards: all-syncro gearboxes for every model, interior door handles instead of strings and a new generation with wind-up windows and concealed door hinges. Yet for all the improvements, some would say that the Mini, like the Sixties, was losing its way.

But only some. If you believed in the simple purity of the original car, the best was already over. If you wanted your Mini to be a shrunken clone of everything else, stick around. In 1969 you could have the Clubman, with its new, ugly nose, 'improved' trim, bigger seats and nearly conventional dashboard. The Mini 1000 replaced the MkII Super de Luxe, extending the 'chic' of hidden hinges and wind-up windows. The first Monty Python was broadcast in October, and Leyland had its own little laugh with the launch of the Clubman-bodied, Rostyle-wheeled, single-carburettored 1275GT. America could now put a man on the moon, but British Leyland couldn't see that the GT wasn't as sporty a deal as a Cooper. Even John Lennon and Yoko Ono stayed in bed to avoid it.

1969, and the Swinging Sixties went their way with Woodstock, the Stones in Hyde Park, Dylan on the Isle of Wight, colour television for the UK, the maiden flight of Concorde, the fifty-pence piece and the discovery of high-grade oil in the North Sea. The maxi skirt arrived to challenge the mini, and BL launched their own Maxi. It certainly wasn't the end of the Mini, not by a long way, but it was probably the end of the beginning.

Spencer Davis Group's budget didn't yet run to a Wood & Pickett Mini each, but they gave it some loving.

'**Classless**, ageless **fun on four wheels**. The least space in which four people can **travel quickly** and comfortably.'

Sue Baker (journalist and former Motoring Editor of the **Observer**,

broadcaster and former **Top Gear** presenter)

chapter five

If the 1960s had been an all-night-party kind of decade, for Britain the **1970s** was definitely the **morning after**. A fairly **grumpy** morning after it would turn out to be, too.

Taste

did the Mini really get better?

It was a decade of strikes and industrial strife, inflation and unemployment, IRA bombs all around the United Kingdom and increasing terrorist activity around the world. A decade of world scandals and political change, from Nixon at Watergate to Thatcher in Westminster.

The new decade flew into Heathrow in January 1970 on the back of the first Boeing 747 Jumbo to land in Britain. It was a powerful symbol of bigger starting to look better again. In a way, that was the theme the Mini followed through much of the 1970s – not getting physically bigger, but trying embarrassingly hard to be a bigger car. It was a mixed blessing. On the plus side, there were real improvements in areas where they were needed – indeed, areas where they'd always been needed. In the late 1960s, the law had forced one change on all cars. *Autocar* summed up what it did to the Mini: 'The compulsory fitting of seat belts naturally caused people to use them, a practice which underlined the fact that the switches and controls had always been about three inches too far away from the driver. For 1968 they were brought just that distance nearer. . .'

Join Our Club

There were big mistakes in presentation, though – some of them merely crass, others far worse than that. It was a time for cosmetic meddling, bright colours in place of bright ideas, and 'special editions' that were rarely as special as the name implied.

The youth of the Swinging Sixties was growing up and beginning to take on responsibilities.

Even The Beatles became businessmen, and officially split up in 1970. That summed up the decade to come – a world without The Beatles. A horse called Gay Trip won the Grand National, but Gay Trip didn't have anything to do with sex or drugs. There were echoes of the past, yet shows like *Oh Calcutta* never had the impact that *Hair* had when being daring was still a novelty. Apollo 13 was saved, but Jimi Hendrix and Janis Joplin died; the partying was taking its toll. In September, Colonel Nasser died, too – the instigator of Suez, the man who had set the stage for the Mini.

It wasn't obvious at the time, but the next generation of motoring chic had surfaced at the beginning of the 1970s, in the shape of the Range Rover. This was a car as different as could be from the compact, economical, inexpensive, classless Mini. It was big, thirsty, cost an arm and a leg, and made class visible again. If you had a Range Rover in the city, it implied your money and style were rooted in the country. If you had one in the country, you were probably something in the city. It caught the imagination of the London smart set, just the way the Mini had a decade earlier. But the Mini had been about fun; the Range Rover was far more smug. It was another sign that that smart set was growing up.

We went into 1971 with yachtsman Heath at the tiller, and storms brewing. Rolls Royce was bankrupt and pounds, shillings and pence gave way to Dismal Guernsey. Hot pants were banned at Ascot and micro skirts made the mini look prudish, but women were asserting a more serious, political side, with Women's Lib.

(Previous Page) 1987 Park Lane – just one of a London names series designed to reflect sophistication.

"As a matter of fact, this *isn't* my favourite car of all time."

"This is one of the latest Minis.®

"My all-time favourite was a Mini I bought a few years back. It was tremendous fun. So much so, I got another.

"But I thought you could never recapture the thrill of your first Mini. Until I saw this one.

"They've put in new wall-to-wall carpets, soundproofing, new seats and controls, a new, smooth suspension and they've given it Supercover protection.

"My favourite car of all time will always be my first Mini.

"If your next Mini's your first, you'll soon see what I mean!".

Twiggy

Welcome back to a better Mini.

 **Mini**

From Leyland Cars. With Supercover.
* Mini' is a Registered Trade Mark

By the mid-1970s, it was OK to sell the Mini on memories, while emphasizing how it had changed.

The sexy sell. All front for Clubman-shaped 1275GT (Top), neat rear for Advantage (Bottom, sorry Above).

The body had all the torsional stiffness of soup, the top looked three sizes too big. A Mini was not meant to be a Cabriolet.

Late 1980s Red Hot and Jet Black special editions, pictured with pretty girl and horribly lifelike mannequin.

'City' was a key theme from the early 1980s, shorthand for a fairly basic Mini, sold with inevitable imagery.

(Previous Page) Designer special edition evokes old memories.

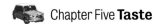

The Apollo 15 astronauts took man's first drive on the moon (it would have been a hoot if they'd done it in a Mini). Nearer home, the government announced plans for a thousand miles of new motorways by the 1980s. It was now easier to buy your Mini too, with purchase tax slashed again, and HP curbs abolished. You couldn't buy a Cooper any more, though. Stokes had called John Cooper into the headmaster's office, and in July 1971, sadly, the first Cooper era ended.

The Cooper's replacement came in the form of the 1275 GT, which had been around since the end of 1969. It was alright if you liked that sort of thing, but with its single carb 60bhp engine and big-nosed Clubman shape, it wasn't a patch on the old shape 76bhp 1275 Cooper S that had gone before. And that was symptomatic of how the Mini changed through the 1970s.

There were real improvements under the skin, but they were mostly details, part of the general scheme of new replacing old. Things like driveshaft joints, gearboxes, gearchanges and so on got better with experience, new materials and the availability of new bits from around the range. Early in 1973, alternators replaced dynamos; a year later inertia-reel seatbelts came along, followed in the same year by the option of a laminated windscreen for the 1275 GT and (on the same car) Dunlop's revolutionary 'run-flat' Denovo tyres on ugly 12-inch wheels – one of the biggest changes thus far to the basic principles of the original Mini, and standard by 1977.

These changes represented the inevitable (and proper) adoption of available technology, but then there was the other side of the coin: change for change's sake. Remodelling was obviously meant to make the Mini more attractive, and by extension more commercially viable, but did it really? Look at the reality. Did tinted glass, reversing lamps, locking petrol caps, matt-black grilles, bumpers and wheelarches, or stripey seats make the 1970s Mini a better car? Did they add anything to the brilliant minimalism of the 1950s Issigonis Mini concept? Of course they didn't. They only made it different.

Limited Special Editions

The decade was unrolling with a tough economy and another round of oil scares. While its advantages of economy and low price should again have become USPs, the Mini's makers seemed more concerned with moving it up-market. That meant pandering to modern expectations. Some, admittedly, were eminently sensible. In 1974, the 850 gained a heater as standard – for the first time! Most changes saw the Mini reflecting the threat of bigger, newer cars. In 1976, for instance, twin steering column stalks, a heated rear window, radial tyres for all, hazard lights, face level ventilation on the Mini 1000, and a host of other additions were offered. In 1977, another mix of convenience and cosmetics: the availability of features such as reversing lights, a dipping interior mirror and reclining seats spread down-range, while matt-black trim and new steering wheels were the obligatory visual updates. A few things were there because tightening legislation said they had to be; most were there because they could be, or because the marketing men said they ought to be.

The most cynical bit of marketing, perhaps, (or the cleverest, depending on your viewpoint) was the new genre of 'special editions'. The Mini 1000 Special of 1975 (International Women's Year and the year Mrs Thatcher became Tory leader) was the first, with coachlined green and white paint, chromed door mirrors, reclining seats, 'Safari' carpets and something Leyland made a speciality of at the time – bright orange deckchair-style upholstery. Which, looking back, tackily defines the period.

Through the 1970s, 1980s and into the 1990s, the Mini spawned dozens of special editions. If you could say anything positive about the new models it was that they echoed (distantly) the golden days of the Mini as style icon. However, the 'style' represented by the 1970s special editions extended mainly to colour co-ordinating interiors and exteriors, mixing and matching low-cost, high-visibility, off-the-shelf trim and equipment packages, and thinking of a snappy name. Whether they reflected the mood of the day is questionable. The year before the Queen's Silver Jubilee saw the birth of punk rock, one-time Mini fans Princess Margaret and Lord Snowdon separating and the worst drought for 250 years.

Apropos of nothing except an excuse for a motoring joke, 1976 also saw the death of Percy Shaw, the man who invented cats' eyes. He had the idea one night on the way home from the pub, when he saw light reflecting from the eyes of a cat coming towards him. If the cat had been going the other way, he would have invented the pencil sharpener. . .

In Silver Jubilee year, 1977, Marc Bolan was killed when his Mini hit a tree; the man who wrote 'Small is Beautiful', economist EF Schumacher, died the same month. To celebrate the Mini's twentieth birthday (and to bring the 1970s to a close as the winter of discontent and more oil shortages paved the way for a new government, and the Iron Lady), we had the Mini 1100 LE. It had metallic silver or rose paint, a contrasting vinyl roof, 'shaded' door stripes, tartan trim, 1275GT style instruments and centre console, and a special steering wheel. Somebody liked it: the planned run of 2,500 was quickly doubled, and the car sold well at £3,300. Even the Mini van (which in the late 1970s was still the UK's best-selling small van, with sales of almost 10,000 a year) ended the decade with a flourish – cloth seats, carpets, passenger sun vizor and sound insulation became standard on the 998, and an 'L' option on the 850.

Failing Footsy

The introduction of sound insulation was definitely a good thing; as standard kit it took the Mini into the 1980s more quietly than it had left the 1970s. Nut and bolt improvements in the 1980s included the spread of disc brakes onto the front of smaller Minis. Mercifully, the Clubman shape was dropped during 1980, and all subsequent original Minis were Mini-shaped. 'City' was the first badge of the 1980s, but City became E, HL became HLE, and HLE evolved again into Mayfair, to keep the marketing men and the badge designers busy. The early Sixties smart-set reference was clever, and was repeated

The Mini Van was introduced in 1960 (when this one was built), ran until 1982, and was always a big seller.

in 1980s specials like Chelsea, Ritz, Piccadilly and Park Lane. The Designer badge recalled the heady days of Mary Quant and Carnaby Street. Advantage had a tennis 'theme' (for no more obvious reason than allowing the PR department to copy the famous poster pose of the tennis player scratching her bottom). Sprite, Red Hot and Jet Black suggested (as opposed to delivered) sportiness.

These were classy, bubbly names for a not very bubbly Mini decade. A decade which, in October 1980, saw the launch of what should have been the Mini's successor, the Metro. It couldn't finish the Mini off. By 1983, the Metro was Britain's best-selling car and Mini production was below 50,000 a year. But it would have cost more to lose it than to keep it. The 1980s saw the shooting of John Lennon, the death of the Mini's great champion Peter Sellers, the marriage of Chas and Di, the Falklands War, inner city riots, stock market collapses, rising unemployment and a falling pound. The decade also saw protest at Greenham Common, the growth of a chip-driven society, alternative comedy, breakfast TV, compact discs, the brief (and much-cartooned) rise and fall of the Sinclair C5 and the miners' strike. There was Live Aid and the stark reality of Aids. The Space Shuttle and Chernobyl both went bang and in December 1986, Supermac died, aged 92.

In 1987 we had the great storm and the stock market had Black Monday, with £50 billion wiped from share values. If there was any justice in the world, the money-market yuppies who had gone from barrow boys to champagne-swilling Porsche drivers and back to jail without passing Go would have favoured the classless Mini. Like their poor but stylish new aristocrat uncles in the Sixties. But the Mini wasn't that fashionable any more. By the late 1980s, a GTi badge was the bare minimum in cool.

Unless you were in Japan, where the Mini was becoming to Tokyo and Yokohama what it had been thirty years earlier to Knightsbridge and the King's Road. As the Berlin Wall came down and the Cold War ended, Japan was the world's biggest Mini market. Without that strange twist, the Mini might never have seen the end of the 1980s, but what kick-started it in the 1960s finally guaranteed its survival into the 1990s and even the next millennium. Style revived the market, and made it worthwhile upgrading the Mini for modern crash test and emissions rules. By the mid-1990s the Mini was selling better than it had through most of the 1980s. Even the Cooper had returned. And the plan was for the original Mini to survive until the new generation arrived in 2000. As it turned out, it was the newcomer that would be slightly later on parade than originally planned; but the original did continue as intended, until October 2000. So there was still hope for us all.

The best way to call the AA in the days before mobile phones. One had to call the AA a lot in the 1980s if one owned a Mini.

'To me the **Mini is to parking** what the **British sandwich** is to **hunger** – a perfect design classic.'

David Bowie (for The Design Museum's 40 Years of a Design Icon exhibition, 1999)

chapter six

While the **Mini** was reinventing the idea of the small car and overturning the **English** class system, it also set about reinventing the idea of the **sports car**, not to mention the idea of the racing car. As a sideline, it paved the way for the **hot hatch** in years to come.

Speed

the authorized version

S'no business like snow business. When the 1967 RAC Rally was cancelled, TV created its own special stages.

Competition success and the giant-killing performance of hot roadgoing Minis surely contributed just as much to the Mini's popularity as the smart set ever did. At the same time, the car's sporty potential created a whole new industry of tuners, preparation experts and after-market goodie sellers, which has survived just as long as the Mini itself.

Yet Sir Alec Issigonis always insisted that he never designed the Mini with any thoughts of it being a sporting car. 'When the Mini was designed and into production,' he said, 'I never gave competition motoring a single thought. We were preoccupied in the design with getting good roadholding and stability, but for safety reasons,

and to give the driver more pleasure. It never occurred to me that this thing would turn out to be such a successful rally car.' Later, looking back on the Mini's sporting glories, he repeated that last thought: 'it never came into my imagination that that little thing would win the Monte Carlo Rally, three times, outright.' But it did, and far more besides.

It's impossible to know whether or not Alec Issigonis was being economical with the truth when he said he'd had no early thoughts about the Mini's sporting possibilities. It's much easier to see that he took a great deal of pleasure from the Mini's race and rally success, and from the roadgoing rockets that gave the car its

(Previous Page) All good, clean fun.

astonishing reputation.

In reality, motor sport had long been part of Issigonis's life, and either side of the war he had been both driver and racing car constructor. In the 1960s and beyond, many rising stars (including future world champions James Hunt and Niki Lauda) would gain their first racing experience in Minis. Back in the 1930s, Issigonis started competing the way many a driver did then, with increasingly sporty versions of the Mini's spiritual ancestor, the Austin Seven. Finally, with his friend George Dowson, he started work on a car of his own design, the Lightweight Special – a slim, beautifully compact, front-engined single-seater, destined for a varied career of hillclimbs and circuit races.

Lightweight Champion

The Lightweight Special used a certain amount of Austin Seven running gear, including one of the most powerful, 60bhp supercharged 750cc side-valve engines, acquired via contacts in the Austin works racing department. Engine and gearbox aside though, it was virtually all Issigonis, and far more sophisticated than the average racing special of its day.

Autosport's famous correspondent John Bolster (himself no mean racing driver, and a bit of a demon in hillclimb specials) described it as possessing 'the appearance of having been built regardless of cost, in the racing department of some great factory.' In reality the project started in the garage of the house where Alec lived with his mother in the mid-1930s, in Kenilworth. When he moved to Morris Motors, the

Lightweight Special moved with him (and mother), to a new house in Abingdon – a town which was then the home of MG, and would later become the base for the Mini works competition cars. The racer was completed, a piece at a time, between there and the Dowson family farm in Worcestershire.

The Special represented classic Issigonis thinking and typical Issigonis design methods – much the same methods as he would use twenty years later on the Mini. Basically, he sketched everything as 'life' drawings, drew almost nothing as conventional engineering drawings and (with George Dowson) turned the sketches into a finished car. Around the same time he also sketched ideas for a rear-engined racing car, but the Lightweight Special was, conventionally enough for the 1930s, front-engined and rear-drive. That was almost the only conventional thing about it, though. The rest was brilliant, pioneering thinking.

As with the Mini, all possible weight was avoided. There was no traditional chassis: the body sides of the Lightweight Special were made of plywood sheathed in aluminium sheet and tied together by front and rear bulkheads, seat, engine, gearbox and rear axle mountings. They were the chassis. Although it was extremely light (the whole car weighed only about 1100lb), it was much stiffer than a normal ladder-framed car. That allowed Issigonis to use softer than usual springing, and also – unusually for a self-built 1930s racer – it had all independent suspension. The final innovative twist, and yet another idea that would eventually reappear in

Alec Issigonis built the Lightweight Special in the 1930s. John Cooper (left) raced against it in the 1940s.

the Mini (albeit in a different form), was that the suspension medium wasn't metal springs but rubber – giving, exactly as in the Mini, progressive-rate springing and a degree of natural damping, with minimum weight.

One other thing you might notice about the Lightweight Special that recurs later. It was a very good-looking car – not because it was styled, just because it was 'right'.

It was finished in 1938 and both Issigonis and George Dowson drove it. It showed its potential by beating the similarly powered Austin works racer at Prescott hillclimb, but the war started before it could achieve much more. It had another life when the fighting was over, and with Issigonis driving it soon started winning again when racing resumed in the late 1940s. And it carried on winning for quite a while, after Alec and George developed an overhead camshaft conversion for it, around 1947. This turned out to be the high spot of Issigonis's racing career; his new bosses effectively banned him from racing by the end of the 1940s – although he later made several appearances with the Lightweight Special at historic events, and the car is still wheeled out occasionally.

The Mouse That Roared

The Lightweight Special has an importance to the Mini story well beyond the ideas it pioneered. It was while he was campaigning this car just after the war that Issigonis met another fledgling racing car designer, one John Cooper. They were both competing in the 1946 Brighton Speed Trials – Issigonis with the Lightweight Special,

Cooper with the first 500cc Cooper Special – for the popular Formula 3 category. Cooper beat Issigonis that day, and they started a long and productive friendship which would ultimately lead to a whole family of Mini Coopers and another side of the Mini legend.

Before that happened, the apparently humble and not very obviously sporty 850 Mini started to rewrite the motor sport rule books. If the Mini's sporting potential wasn't immediately interesting to Issigonis, it was to a lot of other people.

On the face of it, maybe the Mini didn't look like very good competition fodder. It wasn't powerful, it wasn't streamlined, and what about those tiny wheels? On the basis of the first tests with the Orange Box prototypes, its designers had even decided to make it *less* powerful rather than more powerful. They wanted to rein the performance in a bit for the production cars, and for customers not yet used to a combination of front-wheel drive and high performance.

Certainly, as launched, the Mini's 850cc, 34bhp and front-wheel drive didn't have much in common with the typical saloon racer and rally winner of the 1950s. Those tended to have a lot more engine, and hence a lot more power – and that power went onto the road through the rear wheels. But well before the end of 1959 (in fact within weeks of its August launch), the Mini was appearing in competition.

It was no surprise that the Mini's first outings were in driving tests and sprints, where agility and compactness could make up for lack of outright performance. It didn't take long before people realized that they more than just made up. On the racetrack, the Mini could do things with 34bhp that other cars couldn't do with three times that amount. While testing the prototypes, on their road routes around the Cotswolds, the engineers had discovered that they could frighten the pants off bigger, more powerful cars with the Mini's astonishing front-drive handling. On the racetrack, the Mini proved it.

Talking in 1959 about the decision to adopt front-wheel drive, and how that shaped the Mini, Issigonis said, 'a low centre of gravity, good weight distribution, and suspension which comes near to the theoretical ideal led us to hope for exceptional handling qualities, but the results exceeded expectations.' They certainly exceeded the expectations of the big car drivers (and many spectators) who laughed at the Mini when it first put numbers on the doors and ventured onto the track. No, it wasn't exactly fast in a straight line, but show it a corner and the whole story changed. In 1959 (not to mention the 1960s and much of the 1970s) there wasn't another saloon car – and very few sports cars – that could live with a Mini on the twisty bits.

Never were more cars more sideways than in the glory days of Mini racing. Front-wheel drive essentially meant understeer (the front of the car running wide of the intended line as the front wheels were turned into the corner). But by lifting off the power momentarily at the start of the corner, or dabbing the brakes briefly, or simply flicking the car into the bend (sometimes a combination of all three), the rear tyres could be made to unstick and the tail end to come around. Then, by keeping the power hard on, the Mini could be pulled through the corner in a balanced drift. Meanwhile, the rear-drive opposition was lifting off the power to contain their tail-out oversteer. Not only was it a very effective way of running rings round more potent opposition, it was also very spectacular to watch. The arrival of the Mini breathed new life into saloon racing.

Three Wheels On My Wagon

Before 1959 was out, the Mini saw its first circuit racing class win, by popular saloon car racer 'Doc' Shepherd, at Snetterton. But it wasn't all good stuff. Minis had their reliability problems in the early days. These problems were much the same as those of the road cars, but they were much exacerbated by the strains of racing. Exhaust pipes used to break where they were taking the role of lower engine stabilizer and there was always the slipping clutch problem from oil leaking through the crankshaft bearing seal to the 'outboard' clutch housing. Most worryingly, the centres used to pull out of the original steel wheels.

That problem surfaced most dramatically at one of the 850 Mini's first long-distance events, the Six-Hour Relay race at Silverstone – a circuit whose long, fast corners are in any case hard on tyres, wheels and wheel bearings. The Minis in the Relay team lost so many front wheels that day at Silverstone that they were pulled out of the race. The problem was so bad that all Minis with the original wheels were banned from motor sport in the UK. And that led the Abingdon-based Competitions Department to produce

Aaltonen on the 1964 Monte, honourably dirty in the streets, on his way to seventh place. Hopkirk won.

stronger wheels for the Mini racers (the first 'official' Mini competition part), and led BMC to produce better wheels for the production cars.

Once the wheels stayed on, the Minis started winning. After Doc Shepherd had opened the score, Sir John Whitmore, John Aley and very fast lady Christabel Carlisle all added to it – with Whitmore taking the Mini's first big racing title, the British Saloon Car Championship, 1-litre class and outright, in 1961. In 1962, a BMC press ad (headed 'Competition Scoopers, these Mini Coopers') listed the year's successes in 'major world events'. In international racing they included class wins for the Mini in the Coupe des Bruxelles, in the Prix Vienne; the 12-Hour Sedan Race in Washington; the saloon race supporting the German Grand Prix at the Nurburgring; and first, second and third places in the 1-litre class in the Swedish Championship. There was an outright win at Chartre, and, at home, class wins at Snetterton, Goodwood, Aintree, Silverstone, Crystal Palace, Mallory Park, Aintree, Oulton Park and Brands Hatch. John Love had also won the British Saloon Car Championship. In short, it wasn't a bad year. In the following year, Dutch driver Rob Slotemaker, driving a Downton

There were bound to be times when it didn't go quite according to the script. At a Silverstone saloon race in May 1963, Christabel Carlisle, in the Mini, caught up with Peter Harper's Sunbeam Rapier just as it entered mid-accident, helped to shove the rolling Rapier back onto its wheels, and finally parked on top. Both drivers walked away. Paddy Hopkirk is in the Mini that's still on its (smoking) wheels. Christabel Carlisle was to Mini racing what Pat Moss was to Mini rallying, and wrote a book about the car's giant-killing abilities.

Makinen was a genius in the Mini, great company out of it; above, in Monte Carlo after his 1965 win.

entered 'works' car, added the European 1300cc title. Then, in 1964, Warwick Banks scooped the lot, with the British and European 1-litre classes and the European title outright. The same year, John Fitzpatrick won the 1300 class in his Cooper. It was a pure joy to see the Minis on tighter circuits giving those Jaguars and Ford Galaxies an embarrassing time. And yet the most memorable sights in Mini racing were still to come. . .

In rallying, all the greatest Mini achievements were directly down to the works team. However, in racing, the 'works' set-up was slightly different.

The racing Minis were always run by outside teams with works support, rather than directly by Abingdon. The earliest partnership, not surprisingly, was with John Cooper, and Love and Fitzpatrick won their 1962 and 1964 titles as Cooper team drivers.

While the works rally cars always ran the famous red and white livery, the racing Coopers favoured the team's Grand Prix colours, of dark green with white bonnet stripes and a white roof. Soon enough, these two became the only schemes to have for any self-respecting boy racer's hot road Mini.

Paddy Hopkirk and co-driver Henry Liddon in the 1964 RAC Rally. For once, their works Cooper retired.

Champagne And Rosettes

In 1964 and 1965, another future Grand Prix champion constructor, Tyrrell, supported Minis in Europe, albeit using cars built by Cooper. In 1964 they contested the European Saloon Car Championship (and won it with Warwick Banks) and in 1965 Banks added the British 1-litre class win, this time driving for Cooper, while his teammate John Rhodes won the British 1300 class. Always giving both the Cooper- and Tyrrell-run teams a hard time, there was another team sometimes supported by the works, sometimes running solo, but always super-competitive – Broadspeed.

For several years until Broadspeed switched its allegiance to Ford (miffed at not always having as much BMC works support as they might have had) the superbly prepared cars from Birmingham were variously campaigned by team owner Ralph Broad, Fitzpatrick, Handley and others less prominent but rarely out of contention.

The 34bhp days hadn't lasted long, even in the 850 ranks. The first 1-litre Coopers arrived with 55bhp for the road, and very soon 80bhp was about right for the track, in 'Formula Junior' tune. Eventually, the 1-litre racers were delivering as much as 120bhp. Indeed, the fuel-injected,

Not the Monte Carlo; Bob Elice in a Cooper S at Mallory Park in 1972.

eight-port crossflow 1300 Coopers of 1968 were capable of mustering 140bhp – of which some 110bhp reached the smoking front wheels.

Once the Mini racers had power as well as wheels that stayed in one piece, they became especially spectacular when racing each other, team against team, door handle to door handle. None was more spectacular (or faster) than John Rhodes – John 'Smokey' Rhodes, as he was widely known; and you only need see one picture to know why.

Rhodes had the power-on Mini drift down to a fine art, all finely controlled aggression, commitment and wreaths of front-wheel tyre smoke. Fine drivers like Gordon Spice (1-litre class winner in the 1968 British Saloon Car

Championship, for Arden), John Fitzpatrick, John Handley (once he had switched from rallying to racing) and plenty of others gave chase, but nobody smoked them like Rhodes. In the end, he became the most successful of all the 'works' Mini racers, headlined by winning the 1300cc class of the British Saloon Car Championship four times in a row between 1965 and 1968. Even later than that, he scored the works Minis' only major outright race win against unlimited size opposition, in 1969, at the Salzburgring in Austria – by which time the Mini's astonishing ten-year run of major titles was coming to an end.

But it wasn't quite over yet. The Ford Anglias (not least the ones in Broadspeed colours, with

By 1968 the heyday of the works rally cars was over. Makinen and Easter finished 55th in that year's Monte.

Rauno Aaltonen, one-time speedboat champion, motor cycle racer, and the most successful of all the works Mini drivers in the early 1960s.

Fitzpatrick at the wheel) were making life increasingly hard for the racing Coopers, but you could still rarely predict which would come out on top, and the Mini remained untouchable in the 1300 class from 1965 to 1968. By that time British Vita Racing was the other 'works supported' outfit, alongside the Coopers, sharing European and British duties, respectively, in what turned out to be the last year of the works support system – and in 1968 it was Handley and British Vita who won the European title outright.

For 1969, Abingdon officially ran cars of its own, but not because things were getting better. By 1969 Leyland were calling the tune and Donald Stokes was running Leyland. As he would amply demonstrate in his later dealings with John Cooper, Stokes was not a man who understood motor sport – even when his cars were winning. Abingdon got the works racing cars in 1969 (driven by Rhodes and Handley) because Stokes had chopped off the budgets of the other three teams. Cooper managed to put together a team of yellow and black cars sponsored by Britax, but the title was snatched from under the noses of all the 1300 cars by another privateer Mini team, Equipe Arden, and their giant-killing driver Alec Poole in Arden's remarkably powerful 1-litre car.

Even then, the mainstream racing career of the Mini had a final twist in store. In 1969 a one-time single-seater driver called Richard Longman made a name for himself by winning the first motor race shown in colour on British television, at Thruxton, in a Downton-tuned Cooper S. Thereafter, Longman became the man to beat in

Minis. Long after the car's apparent sell-by date, he stuck it right back on the top of the pile. In 1977, racing a Patrick Motors sponsored 1275GT (that's what the badges said, anyway) he won the Group 1 races at Donington and Brands Hatch outright – the first wins in a category that wasn't devised until the Mini's career ought to have been pretty well over. Then in 1978 and 1979 he won the RAC British Saloon Car Championship outright, by virtue of dominating the 1300cc class. In doing so, Longman gave the Mini an unexpected major-league swansong before it finally, inevitably, had to take a well-earned lower profile. . .

Rally Useful Group

In the golden days, though, for all the tyre-smoking, giant-killing antics of the circuit racers, it was rallying that had the greatest impact of all on the Mini's image, and for one famous Mini driver at least, the potential was obvious from the start. John Handley (later that works Mini racer and prolific winner) was almost certainly the first to rally a Mini. Having bought a local dealer's demonstrator on the very day of the car's launch, he took it to a pub meeting of the Hagley and District Light Car Club, and told them he was going to rally it. They laughed at him, but Handley turned out soon afterwards at the Worcestershire Rally, and showed that the idea wasn't as silly as it sounded.

Within weeks of the car's launch, Pat Moss (sister of Stirling, later wife of Swedish rally legend Eric Carlsson), with co-driver Stuart Turner, showed that the Mini could be a rally

The rally début of the 1275 S came in the Tulip, April 1964. This S won first time out, Makinen driving.

winner, albeit in a minor British club event in Lancashire. At the end, Pat described their winning Mini as too slow, and Turner described it as too uncomfortable. Both went on to play major roles in the Mini's rallying career – Moss as the most successful of many female drivers who drove the works Minis, and one-time journalist Turner as the team's brilliant and innovative competitions manager.

The team that he went on to manage was based at Abingdon, home of the MG, and since 1954 also of BMC's Competitions Department. When the 850 Mini arrived at Abingdon it was seen as an amusing contrast to the team's staple rally car of the late 1950s, the big Healey. But nobody laughed at the Mini for long. The first appearance of a 'works' rally version, and the first international outing for any Mini, came in September 1959. It was barely a month after the car was launched, when Stuart Turner's predecessor as competitions manager, Marcus Chambers, took an 850 (one of the earliest production cars, registered in August) on the Viking Rally in Norway. The object of the exercise was to act as a support vehicle for Pat Moss's Austin A40, but in spite of dreadful, deeply rutted road conditions, the virtually standard Mini finished in 51st place.

The works team's first proper international outing came soon after, in November 1959 on the RAC Rally. In one of the first really car-testing RACs, and in weather that was even more wintry than the organizers had hoped for when they moved the event from its traditional spring date, the Rally degenerated into chaos. By that time,

however, the three-car team of 850s was already in serious trouble with slipping clutches (one of the Mini's best-known early problems), and none of them made it to the finish.

They did slightly better next time out, in Portugal in December 1959. Nancy Mitchell and Peter Riley finished 54th and 64th overall, in a build-up to the Mini's first Monte Carlo Rally – the highlight of the calendar at the time – in January 1960.

First time out in the rally that was to make the Mini a motor sporting legend, the works entered no less than six cars (all 850s, of course) alongside another half-dozen privately entered Minis. After an eventful few days, both female crews had retired (the Abingdon works team always had its share of lady drivers) but the other four cars, driven by Riley again, Don Morley, Tommy Wisdom and Alec Pitts respectively, took 23rd, 33rd, 55th and 73rd places overall, with Pitts' car a virtual wreck by the end.

Morley (with his brother Erle in the co-driver's seat) gave the works 850 Mini its first international class win in April 1960, and fourteenth place overall, on the Geneva Rally. Patricia 'Tish' Ozanne completed a good outing with second in class, and it was another of the ladies who scored the works Minis' first outright rally win. In May 1962, Pat Moss (who in spite of her early reservations was proving to be just as competitive in the Mini as she was in a big Healey or an A40) won the Tulip Rally – with a 997cc Mini-Cooper.

That first generation Cooper, introduced in September 1961 (and of which more later)

It wasn't what Issigonis had in mind, but this Broadspeed conversion makes a Cooper S even more beautiful.

showed the way the Mini was going, and the way motor sport was going. When the Mini arrived at Abingdon, it could hardly have been more different from the car it ultimately replaced as the Competition Department's rally car of choice – the Austin Healey 3000. The 3000 (introduced as a successor to the 100-6 in the same year as the Mini went into production) was always affectionately known as 'the big Healey'; the Mini was naturally 'the little Mini'.

The Healeys had done the team proud over the years, thanks to macho power and excellent durability. The Mini brought a very different equation. Admittedly, there wasn't a whole lot of grunt to the Mini in the early days (or reliability), but there wasn't much weight either. So although a 1959 production Mini had only 34bhp, it only weighed about 1320lb. Moreover, the early competition 850 Mini gave maybe 42bhp in much the same weight, so they weren't quite as

Office of works Tulip S, 1964. Rules didn't allow bits to be removed, but didn't stop quite a lot being added.

gutless as they seemed. The first Cooper gave 55bhp in standard form, and substantially more than that in competition tune. And when you added on the Mini's almost ridiculous helping of agility and roadholding. . .

At the end of the day, that was what really made the Mini worth all the subsequent effort. The car just needed some power, and there were people queueing up to deliver that – John Cooper included.

King Of The Road

The Coopers turned the Mini into a major league rally car. After it had scored that first outright international win in the 1962 Tulip, the 997 Cooper was the works team's main weapon until mid-1963 and the arrival of the 1071 Cooper S. With the first S, the Mini was no longer looking at class wins, it was looking at outright victories. And one of the most spectacular victories of all was just a few months away.

In January 1964, the Mini won the Monte. How well those two words go together: Mini and Monte. For all the achievements that went before, this put the Mini on a different level. This was the big time, and the team was starting to look the part. Stuart Turner represented a new generation of professional team managers, far more committed to success than to personal popularity, and a wizard with the rule book. Moreover, the team's driving strength now included its share of the Scandiwegians who were starting to dominate the sport. Over the years, many of the greatest would compete in the works Minis, including the Flying Finns Rauno Aaltonen and Timo Makinen – alongside British stars such as Tony Fall, John Handley, Pat Moss and, most famous of all, Irishman Paddy Hopkirk.

It was Paddy, partnered by Henry Liddon, who won the 1964 Monte, in a 1071 Cooper S, registered 33 EJB. It was one of the greatest giant-killing performances of all time and the first Monte win for a British car since 1956. That year, the rally was won by Ronnie Adams in a MkVII Jaguar. By 1964 the Monte was an altogether tougher event, and more in the modern style of competitive rallying, so the Mini's first victory really meant something. In fact, the win meant something to people outside the normal sphere of motor sport as well, because the Mini's David and Goliath win made huge headlines.

Starting from Minsk (the first time the Monte had ever 'visited' Russia, in the days of multiple Monte Carlo starting points) Hopkirk and Liddon struggled to navigate their way to the common start in Rheims, and they were almost arrested for driving the wrong way down a one-way street in France. But in a car which looked virtually standard apart from its special tyres and batteries of foglights, they led the Mini team home to first, fourth (for Makinen) and seventh (Aaltonen) overall, and the prestigious Manufacturer's Team Prize. It was another huge boost up the social ladder for the mighty Mini. . .

Slip Slidin' Away

And boy, did the rallying Minis keep the ball rolling. In 1965 it was Makinen's turn to win the Monte, this time in a snowstorm. Then, in 1967 Rauno Aaltonen made it one win each for the three biggest stars of the Abingdon rally team, when he took the Monte for a *third* time after an almighty battle with Ove Andersson's Lancia. In fact, most people would say the *fourth* time, because 1966 had seen one of the most controversial Monte Carlo results of all, when French politics won the day.

The Minis were given a hard time even before the start. Rule changes (French rule changes) made it likely that the 1966 Monte winner would come from the new, near standard Group 1 category. Super-manager Turner sidestepped that one by getting enough examples of the new Cooper S built and documented in time to run the car in the class. Round one to the Minis. In one of their greatest performances, the three team cars of Makinen, Aaltonen and Hopkirk took first three places overall on the road – a double hat-trick of three consecutive wins and a 1-2-3 finish. Or, according to the French, not.

After the event, the (French) organizers scoured the (British) Minis almost to the last nut and bolt. Finally, after all else had failed, they deemed that the lighting system, which utilized a combination of headlamps and spotlamps to provide normal and dipped beams, contravened the regulations. All three Minis were excluded. Amazingly, for another infringement, so were the works Ford Cortinas. So a Citroën won. No really, it did. . .

The 1967 win, when Abingdon pulled out all the stops with five frontline entries, said a great deal about both team and organizers. The chasing Lancia, though, was a sign of things to come. 1967 marked the Mini's last Monte win. Developments in the sport made the car less competitive against more powerful opposition from the likes of Porsche, Lancia and Alpine-Renault. But the words Mini and Monte will always be inseparable.

The end of the Mini's works rallying career was fast approaching too. It was all but over when Handley had his last works drive, on the 1970 London to Mexico World Cup Rally. Or in his case, London to Italy, where the car went bang. The last successful works entry was in the 1970 Scottish Rally, where Paddy Hopkirk almost signed off with a win but had to settle for second. There were no works Minis in 1971, or ever again.

According to later team manager Peter Browning's definitive book on the works Minis, the most successful of all the works rally drivers had been Aaltonen, with the 1965 European title, eight outright wins and fourteen class wins.

The most successful (and spectacular) racer was Rhodes, with his four consecutive championship wins. Fifty of the 71 cars listed as 'works' built cars from 1959 to 1970 were 1275 Cooper Ss, and from 263 entries in 116 events, they collected 109 major awards. A hell of a record.

Minis still race and rally (and even win) to this day, but those were the golden years. And that statement takes nothing away from the later 1275GT championships, and especially from the hugely successful and entertaining Mini Seven and Mini Miglia series. Nor from the thousands of Minis that have competed in special saloon racing, and every other form of motor sport from autotests to drag racing. It's just that this is only a one-volume book.

More than anything else, what ultimately limited the Mini in competition in the late 1960s was one of the things that had made it so effective a piece of production packaging – the very small wheels. Small wheels meant small brakes and small tyres, and although the brakes could be made to do a pretty good job, the Mini's tyres would always overheat far more than the ones on bigger-wheeled rivals; and overheated tyres rapidly lose their grip. Larger diameter wheels on later cars helped a bit, but as the wheels grew larger, tyre compounds were getting softer, and softer rubber heats up even more quickly on smaller wheels, so for the racing Minis it was back to square one. Or rather, to square zero. But it had been incredible while it lasted.

The Mini Cooper in its element – Monte Carlo in the sunshine, 1964, year of the first win and the team prize.

'The most tweaky, **disgusting**, twitchy little thing – but an **out-and-out winner**... I hated it when I was in it and loved it when I was out.'

Pat Moss (first Mini rally winner)

chapter seven

In 1971, **Autosport** magazine looked back over 12 years of the **Mini**. The story started, 'If ever a car was designed for the **enthusiast**, it must be the Mini. If you don't believe it, look at a basic Mini **specification**, then look at some Minis on the road. . .'

Speed²

power to the people

The magic words. John Cooper's contribution to the success of the Mini went far beyond the nuts and bolts.

They were right. The old line about winning races on Sunday selling cars on Monday was never better proved than with the Mini. And in the Mini's case it didn't just sell cars. More than ever before in the history of the motor car, Mini owners bought the car, then cried out for all the bits to make it look, sound and go like the ones they'd been watching on the racetrack or the forest stage. When the Mini became a fashion statement, a whole industry was born. When it became a sports car, the industry added another dimension and the tuners and go-faster goodie merchants sprang up like wildfire. Which takes us neatly back to those early days with Cooper and Issigonis.

In the early 1950s, Alec Issigonis's employers more or less told him he had to stop racing. He was simply too valuable as an engineer to be jeopardizing his neck on the race track. Around the same time, John Cooper turned racing car design around – by putting the engine behind the driver. Cooper proved it worked by winning everything there was to win, first in Formula 3, then Formula 2, sports cars, and eventually in Formula 1. On his way to winning two Formula 1 world championships, John Cooper also became a very successful commercial constructor of racing cars, providing the first step on the racing ladder for drivers such as Stirling Moss, Jack Brabham, Bruce McLaren and Graham Hill.

(Previous Page) 1969 Austin Cooper S 1275, the real item.

Just Like That

It was John Cooper who encouraged the rule makers to develop Formula 3 from 500 to 1000cc in the late 1950s (via Formula Junior), and to base the formula on series production engines with a limited amount of modification. He had already identified the BMC A-Series engine as his own choice, partly through his contacts with Issigonis. By the time the Mini was finally launched, Cooper was very familiar with its engine.

Of course, his own cars were famous for having brought the mid-engined layout to Grand Prix racing, while the Mini was equally famous for having brought front-wheel drive to proper road cars. That didn't stop Cooper recognizing the Mini's potential. Almost as soon as the Mini was on the road, several of his star drivers (even the Cooper Formula 1 drivers Bruce McLaren and world champion Jack Brabham) had them as road cars, so it came as no surprise that Cooper began to give the Mini versions of the engines he knew so well from his Formula Junior cars. That was the start.

It wasn't only for the fun of having a faster road car. BMC was already becoming interested in the Mini's competition potential, and Cooper knew that to have a bigger engined Mini that still satisfied the production car rules, it had to be built in numbers (a minimum of 1,000 cars) that were much too big for handing out to the odd racing driver. Too big, even, for BMC to consider, unless they could put the car onto the open market. So around 1961, Cooper suggested to Alec Issigonis that they should build a production version of the Mini with more power and performance. And although Issigonis was apparently unconvinced, he did pass the idea on – to enthusiastic BMC managing director George Harriman, who told Cooper to take a car away and work on it.

Cooper then put something akin to a Formula Junior engine under the bonnet. It was the same A-Series block, but thanks mainly to a longer stroke, it had a capacity of 997cc instead of the Mini's 850cc. It also featured twin SU carburettors, a modified cylinder head and a three-branch exhaust system. The way to performance, then as now, involved three elements: bigger capacity, better breathing and more revs. More fuel and air in, more often, equals more power out. Cooper also swapped the 850 Mini's long gearstick and vague change for a remote shift with a much crisper action. And he co-operated with Lockheed to give the Mini its first ever disc brakes – which, at just seven inches diameter, were the smallest disc brakes in the motoring world at the time.

Cooper took the modified car back to Harriman, who did exactly as Sir Leonard Lord had done with the prototype of the standard Mini not so long before. He drove it very briefly, decided that it was just the thing, and said that they simply had to produce it, even though he wasn't convinced they could sell the 1,000 cars that were needed for racing homologation. BMC also agreed to pay John Cooper a royalty of £2 for each car that they built to his spec and bearing his name, and the first Mini Cooper was introduced in September 1961. In later years,

Issigonis packed a quart into a pint pot, John Cooper squeezed in another gallon. The 1969 Cooper S 1275.

Cooper was always delighted to point out that they eventually built 150,000 Coopers of one sort or another – and that was before the 1990s versions came along.

With 997cc, 55bhp and a closer-ratio gearbox, the first Mini Cooper offered a major performance leap. Top speed was up by more than 15mph, to 88mph, while 0-60mph acceleration times came down spectacularly, from early quotes of around 30 seconds (which in 1959 had actually been considered lively!) to less than 18 seconds. All of a sudden, the Mini had become a very different animal indeed...

Sssss...

There was a lot more to come. The next Mini Cooper, and some would say the most refined performer of all, was the original Cooper S, launched in March 1963. Given the success of the original 997 car, John Cooper commented, 'It had become apparent that the Mini Cooper wasn't a joke. It was a winner... It was a family motor car but it was recognized that with more power and better brakes it could do even better.' So the first Cooper S had a bigger capacity again (1071cc, to fit the 1100cc racing regulations), and a lot of exotic parts like special pistons, valves and valvegear, that were all good for the racing versions. The improved capacity came from increasing the bore (just about as far as it would safely go, involving a new cylinder block with the bore centres moved slightly) while leaving the stroke as short as it was on the 850. That made the first Cooper S a bit of a screamer by early Mini standards – and smoother than a very smooth thing.

The first S also incorporated a further strengthened gearbox, wider wheels, and with them better brakes – still with rear drums but with slightly thicker, slightly bigger diameter front discs and introducing a vacuum servo unit. The improved brakes were without doubt a useful item for the 1071 S. For the road it took power up to 70bhp, top speed to almost 95mph, and 0-60mph time down to less than 13 seconds.

And why 'S'? Apparently, when John Cooper first suggested the bigger, quicker Cooper to George Harriman, the BMC boss wanted to call the car a Mini Cooper Special, but Cooper was dead against that, so they eventually settled on just the initial, 'S'.

In 1963 terms, the original Cooper S had become a very quick car indeed. To put it into perspective, BMC's 'real' sports car with the A-Series engine, the 1098cc Austin-Healey Sprite MkII (and its cousin the MG Midget) only had 55bhp. In spite of having a bigger engine, two seats and a rather sleeker shape than the Mini, it was only good for 88mph and 0-60 in a relatively leisurely 18 seconds. Oh, and while we're at it, the Mini handled better.

Driven forward by competition needs, the Cooper variants came thick and fast. In January 1964, the original long-stroke 997cc Cooper was replaced by the shorter-stroked 998 Cooper, which had the same 55bhp but a bit more torque. It was a bigger leap than 1cc might suggest, because the new engine (based on the 998cc unit for the Riley Elf and Wolseley Hornet) was a lot stronger and more receptive to tuning.

On the good news/bad news side, soon after the 998 Cooper was introduced, so was Dunlop's superb new radial Mini tyre, the 'must have' SP41. That improved grip and handling quite markedly. Unfortunately, six months after that, the Coopers were given Hydrolastic suspension, which didn't do either, although it may well have improved ride comfort. As it happened, Hydrolastic lasted until June 1971, and so, coincidentally, did the first generation Coopers, so by the time Minis moved back to rubber, the Cooper was gone.

Before that, though, the most famous was still to come. In 1964 the Cooper S briefly became a three-car family of Cooper Ss, as 970 and 1275cc versions were introduced, sandwiching the original 1071. The purpose was to cover the 1-litre, 1100 and 1300 racing classes, and the catalyst again was John Cooper. With the 1071 S launched, he was soon thinking ahead: 'I went back to BMC when there was a board meeting going on and suggested that we have a real go a the competition. I said what we have to do now, having had a year with the 1071 S, is build a 1000cc car for the European championship and a 1275 version as the ultimate.' Which, of course, is exactly what he did.

The three S engines all had the same bore, with different strokes, from the very short 970 to the very long 1275. So the 65bhp 970 was the latest high-revving screamer, but the rather less frantic and far more flexible 76bhp 1275 was the one that survived longest and became the most famous. At first, George Harriman reportedly told John Cooper that it simply wasn't possible to get 1275cc out of the existing block, although Cooper already knew that it was. But as Cooper was on his way out, Harriman put his arm around him and said, 'We're bloody well going to do it, though!'

So the 1275 was launched in April 1964 and the capacity survived until the end of the original Coopers in 1971 – and into the 1275GT which, with its single carburettor, wasn't the same thing at all. The 970 was introduced in June 1964, but only survived until early 1965, and the 1071 was dropped in August 1964. Not complicated at all, really, is it?

The 970 S was only made in tiny numbers. Officially, not quite 1,000 cars, even though that was the magic number for racing homologation. It was another very quick Mini, nudging closer towards the 100mph mark and with 0-60mph not very far behind the 1071 S, comfortably in the 13-second bracket. The catch was that it wasn't a car for everyday use. But the opposite end of the new Cooper S scale definitely was.

That was the 1275 S, the big one in every respect. It was the most powerful production S, with 76bhp, and it was the torquiest, with a very strong 79lb ft – way better than any of the earlier Coopers, and heading for twice the original Mini's 44lb ft. So the 1275 Cooper S was a flier by any standards. *Autocar*'s 1964 road test showed a max of over 97mph and 0-60mph in 11.2 seconds; some even more lead-footed testers subsequently claimed sub-11-second 0-60 times. The 1275 S was quick, it became an incredibly successful competition car, and (long before the hot hatch era) it was the hottest of hot properties as a road car, accounting for the vast majority of S sales.

Yet for all the household name status, Cooper remains only the tip of the fast Mini iceberg. For every Cooper or Cooper S sold, nearly forty standard Minis of every variety hit the road. It's just that a lot of them weren't standard for very long.

Home Cooking

The Mini didn't actually invent bolt-on performance – even its ancestor the original Austin Seven had quite a few go-faster options; but the Mini raised it to new heights. The fact is that the basic car was affordable, so was a certain amount of added power, and bolt-on tuning was fairly straightforward even for the average home-garage enthusiast.

You didn't even have to delve inside the engine. The original Mini didn't breathe very well, so there was power to be had simply from changing the carburettor and exhaust plumbing.

Classic simplicity, in the 1965 Cooper S. Smaller leather rimmed wheel and leather seats were after market.

1997 Cooper, with big wheels (Left), and alternator, injection and electronic ignition under bonnet (Above).

If a ten-minute-swap 'straight-through' big bore silencer didn't in itself turn your Austin 850 into a Monte winner, at least it sounded butch and looked sexy.

You could also bolt real power onto a Mini. Once you'd done the ins and outs (the carb, inlet manifold and exhaust), there was power to be had from improving the cylinder head, raising compression ratio, increasing valve sizes, lightening the valve gear, changing the camshaft, changing pistons, changing the timing gears, changing the distributor – indeed, changing pretty much anything. It helped keep it in one piece if you attended to details like a strong enough crankshaft, but it was quite possible (if you tried too hard) to wind up with either less power than you started with or a car with such a narrow power band that it was undriveable. It helped if you did some of the other things too: uprated brakes, suspension, wheels and tyres, engine mounts. But there wasn't much excuse not to make a proper job of it. The other industry that grew up in the 1960s around Mini tuning was telling people how to do it.

Cars and Car Conversions magazine became something of a tuners' bible, and columnists David Vizard and Clive Trickey became founts of all knowledge on DIY Mini tuning, then and for generations to come. And while 'Triple C' died and the new MINI replaced the old Mini, its sister publication *MiniWorld* took up the mantle for those whose love was still for the original. So its specialist book ads continued to offer *How to Modify Your Mini* (Vizard), *Tuning BL's A-Series Engine* (Vizard) and *Tuning the Classic Mini*

(Trickey). Look in the nuts-and-bolts ads and you'll see a lot that hasn't changed, either – more sophisticated maybe, but essentially the same. Stage One kits still have exhausts, carbs and inlet manifolds. There are people who'll sell you bright yellow radiator hoses and frighteningly red rocker covers, but you can still buy real stuff like heads and cams and rockers and timing gears off the shelf. Even the same magic numbers still work: 649 cams, 12G295 cylinder heads, HS and DCOE carbs, BG needles and red springs, are as recognizable today as they were in the 1960s. Which is all part of the legend.

And if you couldn't do it yourself, there were some very good people who could do it for you. The history of Mini tuning is peppered with famous names: Speedwell, Taurus, Janspeed, Oselli, Broadspeed, Longman, Yimkin. Yimkin? I love that one. It was one of *Autocar*'s early pieces on a modified Mini, in 'Improving the Performance of Popular Cars'. The Yimkin Stage One kit cost £18, plus £3.10s if you wanted them to fit it (they were based in Sloane Street, which seemed most appropriate for the Mini in 1961). The kit had a modified, higher compression head and a new SU carburettor needle. It put top speed up by about 5mph and brought 0-60mph down by more than five seconds. Twenty-two quid's worth of Taurus Stage One kit in 1963 hacked 7.4 seconds off an 850's 0-60 time, and twenty-eight quid took four seconds off a Mini Cooper's. The one thing about improving early Minis was that you really could see the difference. . . The serious stuff was pretty serious. Speedwell's 1963 Mini Cooper was a lot more

After a career as one of the most successful Mini drivers, Paddy Hopkirk became the big name in accessories.

Rover called this 1994 limited edition Mini Cooper Monte Carlo. That would be Monte Carlo out of season .

ambitious, with 1150cc capacity, alloy head, special pistons, new valve gear, bigger twin SU carbs, lightened and balanced everything and strengthened bearings. It cost £200 (it also had extra instruments, new seats and so on) but it would run rings around the Cooper S of its day. Its best one-way speed was a remarkable 107mph (over 13mph faster than the S) and 0-60 took just 10.4 seconds. It was a rocket.

Downton, Where All The Lights Are Bright

In those glory days, nobody was better than Downton, though, and Downton is still a name that real enthusiasts whisper with respect. Downton was the village in Wiltshire where the company was based. Daniel Richmond was the man. Before the Mini he was a preparer and restorer of classic sporting cars, from Allard to Bugatti. He became a great friend of everyone who was anyone in the Mini story, including Issigonis, Moulton, Cooper, and Harriman. As a Mini tuner Richmond was a genius – not only for extracting power but also for refinement and reliability. He did his first Mini in 1959, generally did them to order, and frequently for special customers, or as part of the packages from coachbuilders like Radford or Wood & Pickett.

Off-the-shelf customizing. Rover's 1997 Mini Hot Rod was billed as 'the fastest accelerating roadgoing Mini'.

It was amazing that someone as shy and modest as Richmond could list the likes of Steve McQueen, Lord Snowdon, the Aga Khan, Enzo Ferrari, and Peter Sellers among his customers.

John Cooper was one too. It was Richmond who devised most of the Cooper engines, and prepared the most successful ones for the Abingdon Competitions Department. Downton was probably also the first to create genuine 100mph road Minis, but even the way the conversions were described was understated and terribly old-school British – like one of the very late Downton Number 5 Touring Conversions, for a 1275 Cooper S, which, according to one happy owner, 'improved the car beyond my wildest dreams'.

Sadly, Daniel Richmond died young, in his mid-forties, but his cars are one fitting epitaph, and the Mini tuning and racing business is another. Jan Odor, founder of Janspeed, started his career with Daniel Richmond; so did Richard Longman, and Gordon Spice. . .

Not every idea worked as well as Downton's. Bigger engines were clearly a way to more power, so 1275 usually became 1293 when you wanted to steal a bit but stay inside the 1300 limit. Then you could get a bit more out of the standard Mini block by juggling the bores and strokes, moving bore centres around and enlarging the cylinders until the walls were as thin as silver paper. Some were (and are) better at it than others. Or at least better at getting what's left of the engine to stay in one piece. Eventually, 1400 or 1430cc became over-the-counter stuff, but the geniuses could get considerably more. Richard Longman (the tuner turned racer who turned back into one of the world's leading Mini tuners) did one of the biggest ever, a 1630cc monster for an oval-circuit racer in Australia who ran it on methanol. 'It fell in half, I think,' said Longman.

Power Mad

The biggest and probably strangest of all was a lot bigger than that, but it wasn't exactly A-Series based. Late in 1964, the British Vita people came up with an 'E-Type eater', the Mini Buick. Yes, Buick. This monster was built by Harry Ratcliffe and BRT Developments in Rochdale and it was about as wacky as they come. It had a 3.5-litre Buick V8 giving around 220bhp, and it was still front-wheel drive, although the engine was in the back. It had big, six-and-a-half-inch wide 13-inch diameter wheels on the front, but fairly standard 5.2 x 10-inch ones on the back. It wasn't terribly pretty. . .

Mini ace Ratcliffe took it testing at Oulton Park and told reporters it was very fast in a straight line and had so much torque that it only needed two gearchanges per lap where a racing Cooper took eighteen or twenty. He also mentioned that it understeered fairly badly, and snaked violently under acceleration and out of corners. His best lap, in two minutes ten seconds,

was nine seconds adrift of John 'Smokey' Rhodes' 1300 lap record. Harry summed it up drily: 'at the moment the handling isn't all it might be.'

Other hybrids were much more successful than the Mini Buick. With a lot of cutting and shutting you could coax all sorts of engines under a Mini bonnet, including oddballs like the Mazda RX7 rotary. But the favourite ones are various Fords and, for special saloon racing, notably the Ford BDA – an engine more normally seen in the backs of assorted sports cars and single seaters in the 1960s and 1970s.

For a while, Longbridge took an even stranger tack. If one engine wasn't enough, go for two. This time, it probably did start with Issigonis. But not, initially, with an eye to performance. In August 1964, BMC would launch the Moke, the spartan but cute Mini-as-Jeep. Long before it was introduced, in the unusually heavy snows of the previous winter, Issigonis built himself a special one, with a 950cc engine in the front, driving the front wheels, and an 850 in the back, driving the rears. It was shown to journalists who'd been invited to a preview of the real Moke, and also to John Cooper. Issigonis was like a kid with a new toy, delighted at the workhorse possibilities of a four-wheel-drive Moke. Cooper's interest was also fairly obvious, but in a twice-as-powerful Mini. Thus a project started for Issigonis and Cooper to build a twin-engined Mini saloon each, because that's how things happened around these two in those days.

Issigonis's Longbridge-built interpretation had around 110bhp, with one of the engines

The main problem with trying to turn the Mini into a sports car was the tiny wheels, but Ogle wasn't as ugly as most.

where the back seat used to be and a 13-gallon fuel tank in what was normally the boot. There was a scoop ahead of one rear wheel arch to get air in, and one by the other arch (and another in the boot lid) to get it out again. There were two starter buttons, two (linked) gearlevers, and two each rev-counters, oil pressure and water temperature gauges. Issigonis said that he wanted a degree of rear steering to balance the inherent oversteer. Journalist Harold Hastings drove it and didn't say much about the handling, but it did reach 110mph. Issigonis called it the Mini Toucan (as in Two Can). He described it

affectionately as 'the little puppy with the big feet that he must still learn to control.'

John Cooper just beat his friend to the first run of his Twin Mini, and it sort of reflected where he was thinking of going. This one had 156bhp, from two tuned Cooper engines. One gave 75bhp and the other 81bhp. Cooper's biggest dilemma was which one to put at which end. The engineers preferred more in the front (where it was easier to cool); John Whitmore, who drew the short straw to test it at Brands Hatch, said he'd prefer more power in the back. But that's racing drivers for you. It never ran spot on at Brands, but even with the engines out of sync it was quick enough for Whitmore to talk the Competitions Department into building a version to take to the Targa Florio road race. That had two Downton-tuned engines and about 175bhp. On the Targa course in Sicily it was nearly three minutes a lap faster than the fastest conventional Minis (on a fifty-minute lap) but only for a lap at a time, because it had massive cooling problems.

Another racing driver, Paul Emery, also built a twin-engined Mini. Emery was a man very much in the Cooper mould, who later became famous for special Imps, but like Cooper he built various single-seater racing cars, including the Emeryson Formula 1 car. He didn't have Cooper's success, but he didn't have Cooper's backing either, and a lot of people (author included) respected Paul nonetheless. His twin Mini was standard at the front, with another Mini engine and subframe grafted into the rear, with its steering arms locked. The thorny problem of synchronized gearchanging was handled by aircraft-type sleeved cables linking the gearshifts. Emery's own car was intended for GT racing and had around 200bhp (or nearly 300bhp/ton) from two Cooper engines. He also planned to offer a roadgoing saloon conversion, and possibly a twin-engined, Mini-based glassfibre-bodied 150mph roadgoing GT car, in kit form. Sadly it didn't happen.

In fact the 'mainstream' Twin Mini saga came to an abrupt and almost tragic end when John Cooper had a massive accident while driving his prototype on the Kingston Bypass, near his Surrey base. Cooper was seriously injured; the project was killed. George Harriman immediately put a stop to what had potentially been the Mini's passport into another decade of rallying success against the most powerful opposition. The risk wasn't worth the possible rewards. Most other twin-engined experimenters tended to agree.

Fortunately, back in the real world, there were always better options. And for the original Mini there still were, at least for a while longer. By 1999, for example, forty years on from the day the Mini was born, very little had changed for the original generation. The enthusiast magazines were still filled with everything you could ever need to make your Mini go faster and stop harder, and you would still have been hard pressed to find any two Minis that were exactly the same. Even Mini Coopers had become official again, and 1999 saw the launch of two very special models: the Cooper S Works Touring and the Cooper S Works 5 Sport. Both had 90bhp 1275 engines. The Touring had a four-speed gearbox and 12-inch wheels, the 5 Sport a five-speed and 13-inch wheels. They both had sub-ten second 0-60 times, and the classic, white striped, white roofed Cooper livery. They were real Coopers.

And perhaps the greatest thing of all: when the 'new Mini' for the new millennium was unveiled, it had red and white paint. And Cooper badges. Lord Stokes, eat your heart out.

Even in the 1990s the Mini was still a film star. Unfortunately the film was The Avengers, *which bombed.*

'When first produced at a **race meeting** it was greeted with **uproarious laughter** from everyone. This was reduced to quiet chuckles when the crowd noticed how the car went round corners, and changed yet again to gaping amazement when it began to **pass larger cars on the straights**, round bends, and at every conceivable point where it could just squeeze by.'

Christabel Carlisle (early Mini racer, author of **Mini Racing**, 1963)

chapter eight

On 1 September 1959, six days after the Mini was unveiled, **production was halted** by an unofficial strike. Through much of the car's life, industrial **strife** was normal in the British motor industry; nowhere **more so** than in the bit that made the Mini.

Money

how the Mini struggled to make any

In 1959, that meant the British Motor Corporation, formed in 1952 by the merger of Austin and Morris. In 1966 BMC merged with Jaguar to form British Motor Holdings. In 1968 BMH merged with the Leyland Motor Corporation (which already included Standard-Triumph and Rover cars) to form the British Leyland Motor Corporation. In 1975, on the verge of extinction, BLMC was nationalized as British Leyland. BL begat BL Cars, BL Cars got into bed with Honda, and in 1987 BL and Honda begat Rover Group, which was snatched from Honda a decade later by BMW, already with an eye on Mini's future...

Every one of them found it difficult to make money from the Mini, even when they were making Minis by the shedload - and enjoying a product life, with few really expensive tooling changes, that most manufacturers would have killed for.

There was a fundamental flaw in the Mini profit equation. The car was underpriced. Making it so small involved clever engineering. Expensive engineering. But BMC priced it to compete with the cheapest Ford, the old-fashioned, easy-to-build Popular. Not even against the new, more expensive Anglia. Ford took an early Mini, dismantled it and costed it. Their verdict was that at £497, BMC must lose £30 a car. Ford's policy was to cost a car to the penny, save as many pennies as they could, then price the product. BMC's was to think of a price, cost the car, then fiddle the costs – not the pricing.

Got To Pick A Pocket Or Two

A BMC price was always set to compete with the cheapest rival, but that couldn't possibly work with something as expensive to build as the Mini.

The slightest rectification problem in production added build cost; with a complex and hastily designed new car, on new production lines, there were plenty of problems. Worse, it was totally unnecessary. BMC could easily have charged a premium price for a car so technically advanced and, perversely, they may well have sold more Minis if they had.

Selling Minis, however, wasn't the real problem for most of the car's life. Once over its slow start, it became the company's best seller until it was overtaken by its larger Issigonis-designed cousin the 1100, in the mid 1960s. Nominally at that time, the Mini was making about £35 profit per car, but the equation was never that simple.

Twenty years after the launch, *Motor* magazine asked if it was true 'as has been suggested, that the Mini still does not make a profit?' This was the answer. 'Working out model line profitability is not a straightforward question. It depends on how you allocate a proportion of the company overheads to that model. If you just look at the direct costs of producing the vehicle, compared to its selling price, then the Mini is substantially profitable, making several hundred pounds per unit. By any normal commercial method of working it out, the Mini is profitable, but if you penalize it with a proportion of overheads related to its volume, then the profitability is very low. If you work out what the profitability of the company would be with and without the Mini, allowing for the facilities you could get rid of by not having it, then on that basis the Mini is profitable'.

In other words, it depends on whether or not you take into account having somewhere to build it.

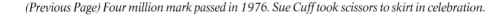

(Previous Page) Four million mark passed in 1976. Sue Cuff took scissors to skirt in celebration.

A 1975 Mini with engine running, doors open...no-one wants to steal it. A perfect allegory for the state of BL.

Mrs T driving all over the industry in a Metro (Top). Lord Stokes, the Mini's mortal enemy in the BL era.

At least I think that's what it amounted to, but don't quote me on that.

Through the rest of the 1960s and into the 1970s, the Mini did keep selling; it stayed in the UK top five, and it sold in useful numbers even into the 1980s. In all that time, its real price rarely reflected its manufacturing cost, or arguably its value. Maybe once the original mistake had been made, it was too late. Nor did the cost of the Mini change hugely, compared with the retail price index, until very close to the end of the original Mini's life, in the late 1990s. It was offered at its 'cheapest' in the early 1970s, before big inflation. In 1973, adjusted to 1959 values, a basic Mini would have been just over £370, compared to a launch price of £497. It was most expensive later in the same decade, with a comparative price of just over £500 in 1978, as inflation dropped below ten per cent for the first time in five years.

From there almost to the end of the 1990s it stayed below £500 in 1959 terms – at around £475 in 1990 (for a 1.0 City), and £488 in 1995 (for a 1.3i Sprite). But by 1999 the price for the cheapest Mini, the 1.3, had increased to £9,325, outstripping the increase in the retail price index to the extent that by 1999 the 1959 equivalent would have been a hefty £707. At that price, even the 1959 Mini would have made loadsamoney.

The Anti-Sell

There was never a real marketing policy for the Mini, either. It was largely allowed to sell as it sold, with occasional half-cock efforts at re-inventing it when it was still selling too many to be killed off but not selling enough to be comfortable. 'Happiness is

Mini shaped', 'The choice in small cars is bigger than you think', 'Mini: the greatest invention since the wheel', and the abysmally apologetic 'Little by little we're getting there', were all advertising slogans meant to keep the Mini ticking over.

Whisper it, but maybe the British Leyland Motor Corporation didn't understand the Mini at all. One episode tragically illustrates that.

When John Cooper devised the Mini Cooper, BMC agreed a royalty of £2 per car. But John Cooper has said it was simply a gentlemen's agreement between himself and BMC boss George Harriman, with nothing ever on paper. 'Harriman and I just shook hands on it. There was no formal contract. It was that sort of arrangement, based on mutual trust.'

Ten years later saw a different relationship between Cooper, BL, and new man at the top Sir Donald (later Lord) Stokes, whose Leyland background left a deep antipathy for anything harking back to BMC. He was respected as a salesman, but had no experience of running a company as big as BL, and no special expertise in manufacturing. He inherited a group whose financial management skills were at best chaotic, at worst non-existent. He faced the disruptive power of the unions, at a time when he had to make hard decisions about rationalization, redundancies and factory closures. The usual image of Stokes is as a ruthless, uncaring hatchet man, but in the early days he probably didn't prune hard enough – indeed, it is rumoured that he was really much nicer than people think.

Stokes's part in the Mini saga would see him cast as one of the most reviled men in the industry.

Longbridge, 1967. Workers see off the Union Jack painted Mini to the Montreal World Fair. Then it was tea.

Painted into a corner by the unions, Stokes had to do something. Unfortunately, he saw no sales value in competition or performance, or in the halo effect of 'outsiders' like Healey or Cooper. One day he asked John Cooper what his role was. Cooper told him, truthfully, that he was a consultant. Stokes replied that a company employing 150,000 people didn't need consultants. And that (for the time being) was the end of John Cooper's association with BL. In 1971 it was the end also of the Cooper as the sporting version of the Mini. By replacing 1275 Cooper S with 1275GT, Stokes saved £2 a car in royalties, but lost far more in image value than he could ever have dreamed possible.

In reality, it was a small part of the Mini's problems. But at the same time it was perhaps one of the best indications of all that there were times, some of them critical times, when the company simply didn't understand what made the Mini work the way that it did.

That's What I Want

On the face of it, the Mini's time should have come again in the 1970s. By 1972 Britain was struggling; unemployment had passed a million, strikes and power cuts were leading to a state of emergency. Another fall in income tax and purchase tax made cars still cheaper, but bust was shadowing boom as night follows day. Summer saw a shock floating of the pound – supposedly to stop its slide, but in January 1973 the Stock Exchange saw huge falls, and by March counter inflation measures were law.

And another ghost was back. There was fighting in the Middle East, Saudi Arabia cut US oil supplies and there were huge oil price increases.

There was talk of petrol rationing, some garages had already closed because they had no supplies. We had a 50mph speed limit to try to save oil, and massive public spending cuts to try and save the economy. In September 1973, foreign cars outsold BLMC's cars on the home market for the first time. The company was already asking for government aid.

Now came the winter of our discontent. The three-day week ran from December 1973 to March 1974, when Wilson returned to oust Heath. BP reported big North Sea oil finds, but that was jam tomorrow. In February four-star went up to 50p a gallon, the fourth rise in a year. By December it was half as much again. From January 1974 to January 1975, petrol prices virtually doubled. It played a big part in rising inflation, to a post-war record of sixteen per cent by the summer, while the FT index was heading south, to its lowest level since the Mini was launched. Inflation pushed prices up, and for the first time the list price of a Mini passed £1,000. As prices went up, so did wage claims, and wages. By October 1974 the size of the average pay packet had risen 21 per cent in 12 months.

It didn't get better yet awhile. In 1975, inflation hit 25 per cent, unemployment was the highest since 1940. Against a background of wage limits and pay freezes, BL was taken into government ownership. It was surely the only way the company could have survived. In 1976 bankruptcies reached record levels and the pound was in freefall against the dollar, slipping below $2 for the first time and eventually getting down to $1.63, as bank lending rates and mortgages climbed.

It was against that background that Mini production peaked, in 1971, at almost 320,000 units for the year. It never again exceeded 300,000, slipping below 200,000 (for the first time in seventeen years) in 1978, and crashing to less than 70,000 by 1981. On the way, for all the decline, cumulative sales passed two million units in 1969, three million in 1972 and four million in 1976. The fifth million needed another decade, to 1986, and by early 1999, fewer than another 400,000 had been added.

Back in the 1970s, the new Callaghan government was borrowing heavily to prop up sterling. By 1977 BL was threatening to close plants if the strikes continued, and the government said no more money. For the first time, imported cars outsold home-grown ones, and in 1978 new Leyland boss Michael Edwardes agreed a BL survival plan with the unions. But 1979 brought another winter of discontent, with rubbish strikes, petrol shortages, and general chaos, until March brought another government collapse, and May brought Margaret Thatcher as prime minister. And that was the Mini's 1970s.

Through the 1980s, it would be fair to say that it survived rather than thrived. In 1980, the Mini Metro was launched, but instead of replacing the Mini, it ran alongside it. In 1983 it became Britain's best selling car, and Mini production fell below 50,000 for the first time, falling steadily for the rest of the decade. The pound was falling too, bottoming out against the dollar in 1985, at very nearly one for one, in an economy blighted by the miners' strike, record unemployment and, at the tail end of 1987, the Stock market collapse of Black Monday, which wiped £50 billion off share values.

I Am The Resurrection

On 2 October 1988, Sir Alec Issigonis died. He had been knighted in 1969 and officially retired in 1971. His mother, his constant companion, died in 1972, after which Sir Alec became increasingly reclusive, with his health failing by the 1980s.

His death meant he missed something he would probably have liked a lot. In 1989 Rover realized what the Mini had been missing. The car celebrated its thirtieth birthday with a party at Silverstone, for which John Cooper produced a Cooper Mini in the spirit of the old Mini Cooper. Rover liked it, and after an absence of eighteen years, Cooper's company was back in the fold producing kits to convert UK market Minis to Coopers. A year later, the Mini Cooper officially returned to the Rover range, and immediately demonstrated how wrong Stokes had been two decades earlier. A pilot run of a thousand examples was planned, but as in 1961, initial estimates proved laughably conservative. The planned thousand new Mini Coopers were sold virtually at once, leading straight away to production of around 600 cars a week.

From the moment the name reappeared, the Mini Cooper was again the star of the range. In 1991 it was followed up by an equally successful recreation of the Cooper S, and the very latest family member was the 1999 Mini Cooper S Works. 90bhp, 102mph and 0-60mph in 8.9 seconds made that a car worthy of the name. It might even have made a profit. Either way, it was a fantastic way to celebrate fifty years of survival – and it wasn't over yet.

The problem with the Mini was that although the car was small, the engineering was complex, and expensive.

'The **Mini Cooper** is a bit of a cult in **Japan**.'

John Cooper

chapter nine

Through it all, what kept the Mini going for **fifty years** was love. The love of almost five and a half million original **Mini buyers**. And, beyond that, the love of countless millions of second, third or fourth owners, spouses, offspring, hitch-hikers and **race-watchers**.

Love

how the Mini won hearts

Brands Hatch Mini Festival 1967, flower power in the rain, and the author is in that grandstand somewhere.

(Previous Page) Valerie Jane in sheepskin hot pants on a 'Wooli' Mini. 1971 madness.

Those five and a half million original Minis touched most of us in one way or another.

The Mini was a natural first car for many new drivers on a tight budget, but you didn't have to be broke to love it, as so many outlandish cars and celebrity owners have proved. It was a great car to own around busy cities, but it was every bit as happy in the country, and many Minis split their lives between the two. Mine did. It was the perfect car in which to learn to drive, and in which to pass your test. My dad's did the business for me. It wasn't the best car in the world for back-seat fumblings, but it had its moments. And it was a car that really flattered the average driver with its amazing handling, while breaking down false social barriers with its unique style.

Coo, Coo, I Just Want You

The Mini was different things to different people. For those who didn't need to make the Mini sporty, there was the option of making it bespoke. From day one it was hard to find a completely standard Mini. You could glitz yours up with anything from a wooden gear knob to a complete coachbuilder's conversion. The catalogue of early (and not so early) Mini accessories ranges from the sublime to the ridiculous. There were bits to stop your engine moving, bits to make your seats more comfortable, inside door handles in the days when there weren't any and dashboards just like a big car's. For heel-and-toe gear changes there were extended throttle pedals, and remote gearshift linkages to go with them, buttons to take the grille out in a hurry, straps to keep the bonnet down and bars to stick lights and badges on.

You could buy racing mirrors, nasty mudflaps, whitewall tyres, sumpguards and sunroofs. Loads of people would sell you more space. For £28.10s in 1961 you could buy a colossally ugly bolt-on bustle which doubled boot capacity (possibly) and 'Improves the Styling' (I don't think so). You could buy fitted luggage, suitcases-cum-roofracks and early versions of that modern motoring obsession, the cupholder. And surely amongst the silliest, a tent which mounted on the roof, took one minute to erect, and was 'just what you need to overcome the frustration of crowded camping sites, fully booked hotels, etc'.

It wasn't only learner drivers and budget motorists who cut their teeth on Minis. Before kart racing became the standard starting point for Grand Prix stardom, the Mini played its part. Niki Lauda was one famous racer who had his first competition outing in a Mini, and like his career as a whole, it was anything but a straight-forward story.

By the time he was twelve (the product of a wealthy, privileged family background, but already a rebel) Lauda had his first car. It was a 1949 Beetle cabriolet, bought with saved up pocket money and driven around the private roads on his grandparents' large estate. When he was seventeen, and a disinterested and failed student, Lauda was sent to serve an apprenticeship as a car mechanic. But he wasn't very good at that, either. He passed his driving test, went back to college, finally passed a couple of exams and decided to be a racing driver. He didn't even have a usable road car at the time, but he had a plan. Without any very impressive qualifications of his own, Lauda had a friend forge him a graduation certificate, just good enough to convince his family that he was a scholar. With the money given to him by the family for his academic 'achievements', he bought his first roadworthy car, another Beetle.

Lauda was then invited to drive another car, owned by the father of a non-driving friend and, as it happened, up for sale. In the middle of the night, in Vienna, driving too quickly, he hit a patch of ice, lost control and practically wrote the car off. This was unfortunate, because its owner did not know anyone had borrowed it. The friend suggested that if Lauda bought the car, it wouldn't matter. Lauda promptly went to his grandmother's house, woke her, explained the problem, and borrowed the money. By the morning he owned a 1275 Cooper S.

This was only the start. He sold the Beetle to fund repairs to the Mini. Then he met Austrian Mini racer Fritz Baumgartner. Another very dodgy deal saw Niki sell the repaired Cooper S, 'buy' Baumgartner's engineless racing S (although he still had to work out a way of paying for it), and build a racing engine for the latest car in his grandparents' garage. When his parents saw what was happening, he promised them it was just for fun, and that he wasn't going to race. He had his first outing a few days later, in April 1968, with the ex-Baumgartner Mini Cooper S.

He finished third on his first run, won his second, and finished second overall. His parents found out (from Fritz, looking for his money). They told Niki there was to be no more racing. Two weeks later he borrowed a BMW owned by another friend's father, and used it to trailer the Mini to the next hillclimb. When his father saw the results in the local newspaper (Niki had won his class this time), he went crazy. Niki left home and didn't make up the split with his family for several years. He traded in the Cooper S (with more family borrowing and a bank loan) for a Porsche 911. But the Mini started it all.

A Mini also started it all for his arch Grand Prix rival, James Hunt. Hunt, like Lauda, had a fairly comfortable family background, little interest in an academic education, and by the age of eighteen, a burning ambition to be a racing driver. He had no money, but he obviously wasn't as persuasive with the folks as Lauda was with his. He suggested to his father that to send him to medical school would cost £2,500, but he was willing to accept the £2,500 up front and leave it at that. His father thought probably not, so Hunt's first racing car had to be more modest than he had hoped. It was a Mini, and he built it himself. He financed it by working as a labourer, a night porter in a hospital, a day porter in a supermarket, and a van driver for the Civil Service – which probably didn't know that the van was regularly used for collecting Mini parts.

Hunt's car was built in the family garage, and towards the end of 1967 was ready for its first race outing, at Snetterton. Well, almost. The scrutineers weren't impressed by its lack of a windscreen and James wasn't allowed to race. When he was, things didn't get much better, and

"I don't care how many there are, you can't park it here." It was fifteen, in 1966, breaking an earlier record.

Designer Paul Smith's personal spin on the Mini, with trademark strong colours and whimsical badges.

it quickly became apparent that the home-built Hunt Mini was no match for more professionally built opposition – which meant everything else. The best thing about Hunt's Mini was that it provided most of the deposit for his next racing car, a Formula Ford single-seater, and that was the real start to a glittering career. . .

Enzo Ferrari was a Mini fan, too. John Cooper introduced him to them almost as soon as the Mini was announced – maybe even before.

Cooper took one to Monza for the Italian Grand Prix weekend in 1959, with his team driver Roy Salvadori. It was a prototype, and certainly the first Mini anyone would have seen in Italy. At the circuit, Ferrari's chief designer Aurelio Lampredi saw the little car and asked Cooper if he could try it. He disappeared for a long time. When he came back, he was a convert. Cooper has reported him as saying, 'if it weren't for the fact that it's so ugly, I'd shoot myself.'

Paul Smith's own signature interior. Different, simple, and still subtle enough not to spoil a good thing.

His boss, Enzo Ferrari, eventually bought three Minis, including a Downton-tuned car that he used to take into the hills around the factory when he wanted to forget his troubles. Issigonis and Ferrari became friends, and Issigonis used to visit Ferrari, occasionally even being allowed to drive the Italian's prototypes. When the automatic Mini arrived, Issigonis and Daniel Richmond from Downton decided that Ferrari ought to have one. Downton did their usual power-boosting preparation job – but when the car was delivered to Ferrari he politely declined it, because the one thing they had forgotten to do was put the steering wheel on the left. Ferrari wasn't comfortable with right-hand drive. But he was always more than happy with his other Minis.

Bend Me, Shape Me
For some people, the side the steering wheel is on may be the only thing they don't change.

I'll be with you shortly. And then he went and spoiled the looks by painting it pink. People do this to Minis.

In the 1960s, the Mini platform with its tight little package of engine, gearbox, suspension and steering, was a perfect starting point for a mobile advertising hoarding. We saw Outspan oranges and Duckhams oil cans, a Union Jack Mini for the Montreal World Fair in 1967 (Union Jack paint schemes were seriously popular in the Swinging Sixties), even Minis converted into snug little motorhomes. Some students were so poor they had to share Minis, a couple of dozen to a car being the record. The AA and the RAC used Mini vans, the police used saloons, builders and gardeners used the versatile Mini pick-up and farmers and beach-bums used the Moke – although the people the Moke was really designed for, the military, never took to it as a smaller Jeep. There was a long stream of prototypes for cars that were intended to replace the Mini, or 'modernize' the concept, but none of them did, and anyway, they aren't what this story is about.

There are the sophisticated Mini conversions, too. The coachbuilt money-no-object luxury cars from the likes of Wood and Pickett, Radford,

(Right) Thirty years after the Monte hat trick, the Anniversary Concept Vehicle, ACV 30 Mini.

It's a Mini, Jim, but not as we know it. V4 engine, rear-drive, shut the top and you'd never know. Would you?

Hooper, those famous names who made the Mini the fashion statement that made the Mini, if you see what we mean.

There were more modest Mini conversions, even cars where the Mini bits were in the minority. The simplest were mild chop-tops like the Mini Sprint (which could be very attractive when they weren't too extreme) and the neat little fastback Broadspeed GT. There were the ones where Mini provided the mechanical bits and the specialist provided the rest – usually in glassfibre, usually short lived and often fairly nasty to look at. The mid-engined Cox GTM and

front-engined Midas were among the prettier ones. The Ogle and the Unipower nearly worked (apart from the tiny wheels, which never looked right); the Mini Marcos looked like a flea and was almost as fast and agile. The rest were almost all uglier still and some of them bordered on the criminally unpleasant.

Minis have been contorted every which way. Elongated into stretch limos, absurdly widened by the advertising men into the rally-trim Maximini (entered in the Marathon de la Route on the driver's side, the Acropolis Rally on the passenger side, and the Monte down the

Remember this one? John Lennon's Radford Cooper S, slightly the worse for wear, but recovering slowly.

middle!), pulled upwards into a double-decker, turned into a car transporter. Just as enthusiastically, they have been chopped and squeezed. The lowest, the shortest, every Mini mutation appeals to somebody, as is apparent at any Mini gathering.

Those gatherings became quite a regular occurrence. The Mini Festivals started in the 1960s at Brands Hatch; successive anniversaries were celebrated at Donington and Silverstone, and the fortieth birthday party at the latter turned into one of the biggest Mini bashes ever, with a programme involving several thousand far from ordinary cars.

I Will Survive

The Mini became a star of the big and the small screen. It flitted (with Union Jack roof) through Carla Lane's *Butterflies*, driven by Wendy Craig. It had a mind of its own (where its owner didn't) in *Mr Bean*, made the dash to Devon for the first of *Four Weddings* (but not the Funeral), and Sellers worked his into *A Shot In The Dark*. The cream of the crop was its central role in *The Italian Job* – a 1969 film co-starring Michael Caine, Noel Coward and Benny Hill. Filming consumed six Alfas, two Aston DB4s, four E-Types, a Lamborghini Miura and fourteen Minis.

The ACV 30 Mini (real Monte winner in background) gave styling clues to the next generation production Mini.

The Minis that jumped the 45-foot gap in the leaping-across-rooftops scene had to hit the ramps at 70mph. They only did one take each. After they landed they were carted away for spares. British Leyland weren't interested in helping with cars for the film, but Fiat (whose products were the police car bad-guys) arranged for Turin to be closed for the filming. Everybody knows the story and everybody remembers the Minis, not the Fiats and Alfa Romeos. That was just another illustration of how poorly BL understood what they had.

The Mini's greatest starring role, though, was as a survivor. For a while, the Mini was almost dead in the water in Britain and Europe, but there was a lifeline for the car from a very unexpected direction – Japan. In the 1980s the Mini became the hottest motoring fashion item on the block, and Japan couldn't get enough of the car. In 1986 they approached John Cooper (ironically enough, by then a Honda dealer) to produce a performance kit for the 1-litre version of the otherwise very ordinary Mini Mayfair, and Cooper was very happy to oblige. After that, Cooper was reinstated as a regular player in the Rover Mini set up, and no return could have been more popular. It was already known that the Mini would soon be replaced by a new generation, and we'd seen it. It was red and white and it had Cooper badges. Perhaps that was when we suspected it could still be a real Mini.

How low can you go? Seventeen and a half inches if you're Andy Summers. Best not to ask how – rather, ask why.

'In **two years' time** your car will be like a lady's clothes – out of date. My car will still be in fashion **when I am dead**.'

Sir Alec Issigonis (speaking to Italian stylist Pinin Farina)

chapter ten

The very last example of the **Original Mini** left the Longbridge production line in October 2000. If the car's future had still been in the hands of the British motor industry, it would have been the last Mini, full stop. But waiting in the wings, the **Mini** had an **unlikely saviour**.

Faith

how BMW picked up the pieces

1959-2000

Welcome back: the new generation MINI in 2002 – still with Cooper stripes and Mini attitude.

It was BMW who saved the Mini, by creating the MINI – the capital letters being the official way of labelling the new generation. They did it with a degree of understanding of the original that came as a pleasant surprise, but they also did it with a modern spin that was entirely their own. The original Mini was created as a utility car a cut above the usual utility cars; the MINI was created to support BMW's new corporate philosophy of being able to offer a 'premium' product in each market segment they chose to enter.

At the time they committed to MINI, the BMW portfolio included cars from Rover and Land Rover, with Rolls Royce at the top of the pile. But that had already started to change. And as for the MINI, the continuity offered by the Rover connection was about to go.

All this, however, is getting ahead of a story that starts long before BMW, or even Rover, had anything to do with the Mini. It goes right back to the 1960s, when Issigonis began to look at a replacement for the original car – almost 35 years before BMW finally created one. At the time, clearly, no one expected the Mini to survive as long as it did and even by the mid-1960s it had been overtaken (in some ways at least) by a new

(Previous Page) The last of the first, with Lulu to bridge the gap to the swinging sixties.

What might have been. The 9X exercise was BMC's first attempt to replace the Mini, and Issigonis' last.

breed of not-quite-so-small car. So the first Mini-replacement exercise, codenamed 9X, was a boxy design with a hatchback-like rear window, a low waist and a high roofline that gave lots of glass area. It had as much interior room as an original Mini but it was a couple of inches wider and, with almost no overhang ahead of the front wheels, it managed to be even shorter than the existing car in spite of having a longer wheelbase. Not only would it have been lighter, but a big reduction in the number of parts would have made it easier and cheaper to build, even with its modern overhead camshaft engine.

At much the same time there had been other projects that didn't really amount to much more than styling variations and body stretches on the 'classic' Mini theme. These left the mechanical bits essentially unchanged and concentrated on chasing a bit more interior space, while the equipment levels were improved with niceties such as wind-up windows. Not really the Issigonis way of doing things, but an indication that the classic shape was far from finished yet.

As it turned out, in the end 9X wasn't killed by engineering problems but by political ones, as BMC morphed into BMH and then British

Under the disguise, ADO88 starts the long haul towards becoming the Mini Metro, but not a new Mini.

Leyland, who couldn't afford to invest in the idea. So with just two prototypes built, 9X was abandoned as the 1960s drifted into the 1970s. And although Issigonis himself was no doubt relieved that BL's woes would mean his original Mini would live on, sadly the 9X also proved to be the last full-scale project he would instigate.

It wasn't, however, the last early attempt at replacing the original Mini. Project ADO74 started in 1972 as a slightly larger car and lasted about as long as Project 9X, but because of more funding it came far closer to production. Like the 9X, it would have had a new range of overhead cam engines but would have been a bit bigger than the original, as well as more expensive. Several styling suggestions were explored and even costings were worked out. But when BL realised what it would take to put it into production ADO74 was scrapped too, for lack of funds, even before they had built roadworthy prototypes. Ironically, if they could have afforded to build it, they would probably have done very well with it, given how much the small-car market was growing.

Then there was ADO88. That emerged in 1973 alongside ADO74 but, because it would have used existing mechanical elements, making development a lot more affordable, ADO88 hovered on the brink of production for even longer. Long enough, in fact, to become the basis for the slightly roomier LC8 study, which would finally emerge as the production Metro in 1980. Again, ADO88 had been longer and wider than the classic Mini, and it was a hatchback. Those basics hadn't changed much by the time it became LC8, after the company changed again in 1975, this time becoming Leyland Cars, under government sponsorship.

Here was another twist, because having finally committed the restyled LC8 for a production launch late in 1980, yet another new management decided that it wouldn't be a Mini replacement after all; it would be a new model, known as the Mini Metro, and the classic Mini would continue. Which it did.

Now fast forward to the 1990s and a changed world. The company was now Rover Group and the Metro – a successful car in its own right, but not really a Mini – had metamorphosed into the Rover 100. The old Mini was hanging on in spite of production having slowed down to a trickle and, after Rover's flirtation with Honda as technical partner and minority shareholder, BMW were in charge. Early in 1994 they had bought the Rover Group from British Aerospace,

who had in turn bought it from the government at a knock-down price. The BMW move came as something of a surprise to most of the industry, whose sceptics reckoned that Rover was already dead in the water and that BMW had really bought Land Rover (with the technology they wanted for a future generation of off-road BMWs) and taken the rest just to do the deal. But the rest did include, among other things, the Rover brand, Austin-Healey and Riley sports car brands, the MG and Mini. And Mini offered BMW something none of the others could – volume.

Volume (that is, building huge numbers of very similar cars for economies of scale) is one of the pillars of the industry. That was as true in 1994 when BMW bought the Mini name as it had been in 1959 when the Mini was launched, or even in the 1920s when the Austin 7 was the thing. But for years, although BMW had been successful as a premium sporty brand, it had been an awkward size in volume terms – not quite big enough to guarantee long-term independence in an industry where mergers were still a regular occurrence, but too big to want to lose that independence.

They could broaden the reach of the BMW brand itself by moving into niches like 4x4 'Sport Utility Vehicles' with the up-coming X5 (and eventually the X3) and had long-term plans for a small BMW – for want of a better name, the 1-Series. But a new Mini, which would also be a replacement for the Rover 100, would offer bigger numbers and, therefore, an entirely different possibility. By the late 1990s BMW were talking of increasing volume by as much as 65 per

What ADO88 (via LC8) became, the Mini Metro – a Mini by name, but not a Mini by nature.

cent by 2005, courtesy of the X-Series and Mini. In the Mini's case, what the car would ultimately turn out to be was partly about nuts and bolts, partly about positioning. A BMW 1-Series, if it happened, would be small by BMW standards but big by Mini standards. And expensive by Mini standards, because BMW had pledged that even the smallest BMW would always have rear-wheel drive (which defines the classic BMW driving personality but is more expensive to mass-produce than front-drive). BMW also knew exactly how far down-scale it could go and still justify a BMW badge and keep the BMW image.

A Mini, on the other hand, was expected to have front-drive, expected to be small, expected to be keenly priced. In being built by BMW, it would have the added advantage of bringing down the 'Corporate Average Fuel Economy' (or CAFE) figure of the BMW range. That is the official assessment of the average fuel consumption achieved by everything a manufacturer sells, weighted for numbers built and leading to potentially costly financial penalties if the manufacturer doesn't meet set targets. Meeting those targets, for environmental as well as commercial reasons, is part of every

When the real Mini successor did arrive, in the form of the MINI, it had genuine Mini DNA.

manufacturer's long-term environmental responsibility, and the industry was only too aware of stringent new CAFE demands that would come into force in 2008. But the clincher for BMW: it didn't have to be badged BMW-Mini, it could stand alone as simply MINI. That, in the longer term, would become a family in its own right – because BMW had already seen far greater value in the Mini name than Rover ever had. Soon they were talking about a MINI 'brand' that, by the time it reached a second generation of its own, could sell 500,000 cars a year in a segment that wouldn't undermine

BMW's own smaller car plans (to whit, a Golf-sized '1-Series' pencilled in for a 2004 launch). So BMW now had more reasons to do MINI than not to do it.

There were still blind alleys. Inevitably, some engineers had continued to play with the original Mini, as after-hours projects if not as real production possibilities. Some of them were interesting, especially the 'Minki' exercises from 1994. Those took yet another spin – this time the last – on updating rather than re-inventing the 'classic' Mini. Both looked just like the real thing and Minki One almost was, except for a chopped down, three-cylinder version of Rover's admired twin-cam, 16-valve, K-Series engine in place of the venerable pushrod A-Series. But pursuing the grail of K-Series power, Minki Two squeezed the whole four K-Series cylinders plus five-speed gearbox and Rover 100 Hydragas suspension into a shell that, apart from being stretched and widened, would have passed as a 'real' Mini.

But there was now real movement from the new owners. In May 1995, *Car* magazine looked at the future of all things Rover and said this about the Mini: 'BMW is clear about one thing: Rover needs a radical new Mini to replace the present 36-year-old model as well as the ageing 100 (formerly the Metro). Designers and engineers at both Rover and BMW have been issued with blank sheets of paper, and orders to come up with something that not only looks distinctive but is also mechanically advanced. It may be an electric or a hybrid.'

They continued, 'The newcomer will be about the same size as the current model but won't be ultra-cheap. Senior BMW figures talk of starting prices at least as much as today's top-spec Mini. The vehicle may also be sold by some BMW dealers.

'According to a source within BMW, the Mini Mk2 may adopt elements of the BMW Z13 concept car, a radical rear-engined three-seater first seen at the '93 Geneva Show. Although the Mini will probably be able to seat four or five, the controversial space-saving rear-engined layout is being considered. Bernd Pischetsrieder [BMW's man was chairman of Rover in 1995] recently tried the Hydragas-sprung Mini Cooper

developed by Dr Alex Moulton too, although BMW's views on Hydragas are unknown. Mix all this with an unmistakable shape and a high-tech three-cylinder engine, and the upshot could be a very distinctive car that is not alien to BMW (remember the Isetta bubble cars?).'

That last aside was quite funny as the Isetta and its bubble-car ilk were exactly what the original Mini had been created to drive off the face of the earth, but you knew what they meant.

Car asked Pischetsrieder how the new Mini was progressing. He was frank: 'Slowly, because there are a lot of other things to get on with. But there will be a new Mini, and the intention is to make it as trend-setting and as radical as the first Mini. And that's going to be hard.' Asked when it would be launched he said, 'Impossible to say exactly, but certainly not for another four or five years.' *Car* rounded off with another vital question: would BMW have a hand in its design? 'Possibly. However, the Mini is in truth a separate brand, not just part of Rover. And because the British understand that sort of car better than anyone else, I'd expect Rover to play the main part in its design.'

So by 1995, BMW really had committed themselves to a new Mini (or MINI as it would become) and although at this stage there were still competing designs, the project that would eventually win the nod was already underway, and in BMW numbering it was called E50. When it was handed over to Rover the following year and re-named R50, there was some dispute over 'ownership'. But the brief remained to build a car with the character of the original Mini and the

BMW thinking on a Mini-sized car some time before the MINI – the electric-powered sub-compact E1.

'premium' quality of any other BMW. Defining exactly what that meant, though, brought more twists, because the BMW and Rover engineers had been doing different things with their blank sheets of paper. It's interesting to look back on how each was thinking before E50 became the design of choice. It also explains *Car*'s reference to electric cars and hybrids.

Both BMW and Rover had been working on small cars, but strictly speaking none of them had been Minis. BMW's especially weren't and Rover's only loosely were. They were quite different from each other. BMW's small-car thinking leading up to the time of their Rover

take-over was summed up by two concepts, E1 and Z13. E1 came first, right at the beginning of the 1990s, and was more concerned with minimum emissions than minimum size, because at the time that was what was expected – especially by America.

The E in this case stood for electric and the compact four-seater had an aluminium frame, rear-mounted motor and strictly limited range and performance. Z13 was similar in size to E1 but quite different in most other respects, especially performance. It looked more sporty, with McLaren F1-like central driving position and a set-back passenger seat on each side. With

Proof that Rover thinking could be even more radical than BMW's – Spiritual and Spiritual Too.

a rear-mounted 1100cc, four-cylinder, BMW motorcycle engine and continuously variable transmission, it was considerably faster.

It was still no Mini replacement though – not least because in 1993, when it was shown in Geneva, BMW were still a year away from taking over Rover and the Mini badge. One more early 1990s' small BMW concept, combining motorcycle and electric power into a 'hybrid' drive, wasn't a Mini in the making either.

Rover, on the other hand, at least had the spirit of the Mini in mind, as reflected by three projects that emerged in quick succession. The first to appear in public was ACV30, which was unveiled as a publicity exercise in January 1997 at the Monte Carlo Rally. The name stood for Anniversary Concept Vehicle, while the '30' celebrated the 30 years that had passed since the Mini completed its Monte-winning hat-trick of the 1960s. The rear-engined, tube-framed, MGF-powered two-seater was finished in classic red and white Cooper colours, with white roof and bonnet stripes. With the benefit of 20/20 hindsight there were far more clues to the MINI to come in ACV30 (especially in the wildly stylised interior) than we might have guessed. But a couple of months later it was eclipsed by the two Rover projects that looked far more likely to be the future.

The names of the new pair were Spiritual and Spiritual Too. They appeared, together, after BMW had given the go-ahead to the MINI project proper. They were presented at the Geneva Show in March 1997, although they had already been around the Rover design office for 18 months. Not surprisingly, given the timing of their unveiling (and the fact that the outside world was unaware that BMW had already decided where it was really going), they were widely seen as the strongest clues yet to what the new Mini might actually be. They did, after all, carry 'MINI' badges, which was more than any BMW exercise had. So *Autocar* devoted half a dozen pages and a studio 'photo session' to them in the week of their show debut, under the headline 'Mini's big future', with the catch-line, 'It's small, spacious, cute, revolutionary: everything the new Mini needs to be. So is this it?'

The answer, as it turned out, would again be no, but the question was reasonable enough. They were exciting cars and oddly, given the two companies' relative reputations, far more adventurous than BMW's parallel proposals. But it's apparent now that BMW used them at the Geneva Show more as a smokescreen than as a toe in the water. For one thing they managed to steal some of the thunder from Mercedes' launch of their own revolutionary small car, the A-Class. For another, they kept the Mini story on the boil. And with work on the E50 concept already pushing ahead, they mischievously fed speculation such as *Autocar*'s.

That's not to say the respected weekly presented Spiritual and Spiritual Too as the real deal. They didn't; they were far more balanced. Up front they said, 'The car, revealed exclusively to *Autocar* at Rover's impressive new Gaydon technical centre in the Midlands, is not the new Mini being readied for production in two years' time, but a design study that combines elements of that car as well as clues to the look of its replacement – a third generation Mini – further into the new century.'

The cars themselves, created under Rover Design boss Geoff Upex, were intriguing. Spiritual was closest to being a true '21st-century Mini', while Spiritual Too was more of a supermini. Like the original Mini, Spiritual was exactly ten feet long, but wider and taller. It was a three-door hatchback with its small wheels pushed right out to the corners. It looked genuinely futuristic while still having something of the Mini in its proportions and details. There was something of the original, too, in the huge amount of interior space for exterior size. Under the skin it went for maximum innovation – as Upex said, in the true spirit of Issigonis. And with respect for the spirit of Issigonis' car. Upex told *Autocar*, 'We hear a great deal from concerned Mini enthusiasts around the world about how we

Under the skin of Spiritual, clever 'mid-engined' packaging, a wheel at each corner and cute curves.

should go forward. We want to show them, first with ACV30 and now with the Spiritual cars, that we understand the value of what we have and that the future of the Mini is safe in our hands.' This was said, of course, at a time when the Rover Design department thought it *was* still in their hands.

Faced with modern safety legislation, Spiritual pushed its three-cylinder petrol engine (K-Series-based, 800cc, overhead-cam, three valves per cylinder, 60bhp) longitudinally and almost horizontally under the rear seats, ahead of the transmission. With a planned weight of only 700kg it promised low consumption (up to 90mpg), low emissions, 100mph performance and 0–62mph in about 13 seconds. With fuel

tank under the front seats and spare wheel, battery and radiator under the 'bonnet', it had outstandingly space-efficient packaging and room up front for effective crash protection structures. Hydragas suspension, too, would have given it a big-car ride with classic Mini handling.

Spiritual Too was mechanically similar but bigger, with five doors, a longer wheelbase and more room. Upex suggested, 'Think of it as an 1100, compared with the first Mini.' It would be heavier than Spiritual at 900kg but more powerful, with an 1100cc, four-cylinder engine to give similar performance with only a small fuel penalty – but still aiming to be best in class. *Autocar* concluded, 'Do the Spiritual cars contain clues to the Mini of 2000? Rover enigmatically says "not necessarily" ... Nevertheless, we've a strong feeling that the Spiritual twins do contain strong, positive hints of the Mini in our future. Another British world-beater? No reason to doubt it so far.'

That, as we now know, was wide of the mark at least for the second generation Mini, but in a side panel in the story, headed 'What Spiritual tells us about the new Mini', *Autocar* proved to be very close to a lot of future truths. 'Although Rover's Geneva concepts have no direct relationship with the new Mini due to be launched in 2000,' they said, 'the cars add detail about what we can expect. The new Mini will use a transverse front-drive design, using engines built in a Chrysler factory in Brazil.' Correct. 'Be at least 300mm (12in) longer than either the original car (or Spiritual) because of the need to meet crash regulations.' Correct. 'Have a much higher and wider body than the original.' Correct. 'Be designed and developed within the Gaydon technical centre as a Rover-managed product – within a few miles of where the original Mini was conceived 40 years ago.' Correct, up to a point. 'Carry many Mini styling cues, but express them subtly; it is its own car, not a pastiche.' Correct, absolutely correct.

'Further its reputation for being "sporty and fun". Too many cars leave them out, says Rover.' Spot on. 'Be positioned as a premium product, not a car for every man as the Issigonis original was ...' Ditto. '... Rover wants the car to be profitable at 120,000 cars a year.' Very close to BMW's starting point. 'Possibly appear as a range of cars as one of the four company marques (the others are MG, Rover and Land Rover).' Spot on again in becoming a range of cars and, if BMW hadn't sold the other marques off, MINI would undoubtedly have been part of the family. 'Offer a lot of cabin space and use a high seating position and large doors for good access.' Not quite so accurate. And finally, 'Be based on a steel monocoque structure using the Moulton Hydragas suspension made famous on both the Mini and the Austin 1100.' Steel monocoque yes, Hydragas no. Eight and a bit out of ten, though, wasn't a bad analysis.

Yet even as they were writing that, pivotal decisions were being made and the Mini's future was becoming more dependent on BMW than on Rover. By the time Spiritual and Spiritual Too were actually shown to the public, BMW was asserting itself.

As early as 1995 BMW had supposedly decided that, whatever the merits of the Rover proposals (including the Spirituals), the final design would come from within BMW. On the other hand, by 1996 they had made a commitment to place development of the car with Rover – a decision that apparently saw the project transferred to Rover lock, stock and barrel, virtually overnight. The whole process became very contentious, as a brief flurry in *Car* in June and July 2001 (launch time) showed.

Controversially jumping the 'first drive' embargo, *Car* had scooped every other magazine by driving a dealer car and writing about it. They also ran a story about the new MINI's development, which included this quote: 'Rover "wasn't a great deal of help" when BMW was designing the MINI's front-drive chassis. This, according to one (presumably BMW) engineer, was because Rover's last fully developed front-wheel-drive car was the Maestro/Montego series'. In the next issue, there was an incensed reply from a former Rover engineer, Robin Ford, who had been closely involved with the MINI project at Gaydon. The gist of his objection was that while BMW concentrated on getting the looks right, Rover had been given maximum freedom in engineering not only the MINI's suspension but also its engine and gearbox, at Longbridge and Gaydon. Or rather, it had been given the *responsibility* to do so, because, it seems, when BMW handed the technical side of the project over to Rover, E50 wasn't much more than a shape and a broad mechanical outline that needed the substance adding – and at the same time needed to be cost-engineered for full production.

The truth is that it was a joint development, although the bone of contention remained – just how much did each side contribute? Even long after the launch this stayed open to argument, although it's definitely fair to say there was ample evidence to show that Rover played far more than just a last-minute quick-fix role in finalising the look as well as the mechanical specification. There is ample evidence, too, that BMW gave them significant support.

Whatever, Robin Ford also told *Car* that Rover's involvement with the project came to an abrupt end. As abrupt, it seems, as the 1996 decision to give them the job. And it happened early in 2000, 'when BMW suddenly asked for the Mini computer files to be hurriedly downloaded to German hard drives.'

All this, of course, reflected happenings far beyond the engineering of just one car; rather, it was driven by what was unfolding between BMW and Rover on the corporate side. By the end of 1999 both Bernd Pischetsrieder and his R&D chief Wolfgang Reitzle had been ousted from the Rover board and new BMW boss Joachim Milberg was making the decisions. One of his first was to get rid of Rover altogether, because it was losing money big time – BMW had come to think of it only half jokingly as 'The English Patient'. It had realised, too, that with the BMW X5 off-roader pretty well completed, it no longer needed Land Rover either. And so, early in 2000, BMW sold out of the Rover Group entirely.

Or not quite entirely, because the one thing it was absolutely certain about taking with it, while leaving Rover, Land Rover, MG and the rest to their own future, was the Mini brand. The only thing remaining now was to create the MINI car and, even as the sparks flew over the Rover deal, that was coming together.

The hood scoop and other details say new MINI Cooper S, but the whole look still says Mini.

'There will be a **new Mini**, and the intention is to make it as trend setting and as **radical** as the first Mini. And that's going to be **hard**.'

Bernd Pischetsrieder (to **Car** magazine, 1995)

chapter eleven

Few cars in the history of motoring have had a tougher act to follow than did the **new MINI** – and as well as having to live up to everything its predecessor stood for, the **great** British **icon** was to be built by a German giant, in Britain. To succeed, it would have to be very good indeed. And it was.

Rebirth

MINI by name, Mini by nature

It was a sign of the strength of the Mini as an icon that of all the badges in the Rover portfolio, that was the one BMW ultimately hung on to. In fact it did so as assertively as it had fought to own Rolls-Royce at the other end of the scale. Even before they finally bailed out of Rover, BMW had realised that the MINI would be a BMW core product, whereas Rover only ever saw it on the fringes – and equally, BMW saw Rover as the minority marque. But just as Rolls-Royce was the ultimate luxury car brand and BMW itself was in the high-centre of the market, MINI had to fulfil one immutable BMW rule. It had to be a 'premium' offering within its own market niche.

That premium philosophy meant the new MINI would be very different from the old Mini. It also concentrated BMW's mind on getting this car absolutely right – and right the first time round.

The gestation period was long, or at least longer than BMW had intended in 1995 when they committed themselves to the project. But given the commercial upheavals in between, it's surprising that it survived at all. Only when the MINI finally appeared in the summer of 2001, around two years later than originally planned, was it clear that it had been too good to lose.

Spool back to the beginning of the development process. By 1995 it was clear that the proposal that would be seen through was the one that started as E50 and became R50, before finally becoming MINI. Many other things are disputed about the development period, but one thing that's certain is that the look was chosen first. The shape that was to be refined into the final product was chosen from 15 full-sized studies. Five apparently came from BMW Germany, five from BMW Designworks in California, four from Rover and one from an outside agency in Italy. They ranged from something very like the original Mini brought up to date, to designs that were even more extreme than Rover's rear-engined Spiritual concepts. The shape that won was created by Frank Stephenson and was, arguably, the clearest sign of all that BMW actually understood the Mini heritage.

Frank Stephenson himself definitely did, either because of, or in spite of, an interestingly cosmopolitan background. By birth Stephenson is American, but before he joined BMW in 1991 he had been brought up in the Middle East, Spain, Turkey and Germany. He spent only four years living full-time in America while studying at the Arts Centre in California and then worked for Ford in Cologne. Before he delivered his design ideas for the new MINI he also worked on BMW's new X5. In mid-2002 Frank moved as design boss to the Fiat Group, where his work included the Ferrari F430, the Maserati MC12 and, rather ironically, the Fiat 500 – another small-car icon of the original Mini's generation, recreated by the man who also helped recreate the Mini. Via Alfa Romeo, he then headed, late in 2008, for McLaren, to work on their promised new road cars. And of course, in a quiet moment he wrote one of the forewords to this book.

In 1995, when he did the first studies that eventually became E50, Stephenson was in his mid 30s and leading the BMW design team in Munich. BMW made their basic design decision in October 1995 and Frank's design won,

(Previous Page) A new MINI Cooper in 21st-century London – echoes of the Mini's spiritual home.

Hands on design: Frank Stephenson working on a full-size clay model of what would become the MINI.

although it wasn't until the beginning of 1996 that Rover realised the finality of the decision. Looking back now that the car is a production reality, it's clear that it was a good choice.

Frank Stephenson's early sketches already had the feel of the new MINI as it would eventually appear. Considering them now you can see that from the start he had captured the spirit without resorting to a retro copy. When the car was ready for launch he told *Autocar*, 'We wanted the first impression when you walk up to the car to be "it could only be a Mini". We didn't want to grow it into a different class. The objective, as with the original, was to make it compact – to use the minimum exterior dimensions for the maximum interior space. Today's safety and comfort issues impinge on that, though, so we've had to grow the car a little to meet those requirements.'

But in this MINI, the old rule 'size isn't everything' really does work. The chosen design was 'evolutionary' – as in, 'how would an original Mini look now if its shape had been steadily developed rather than being frozen in time?' For one thing, it would simply had to have grown.

People had grown taller since the Mini was launched in 1959. Expectations had also grown

Early Stephenson design ideas, July 1998 – already recognisably MINI but with prominent Cooper cues.

tougher – for safety, comfort and equipment levels, all of which needed more packaging space. But it still had to be what by this time had become accepted as mini-sized, like the then-new VW Lupo, rather than supermini-sized, as in the Golf. Not least, BMW also needed to leave room for their own Golf-sized newcomer, the 1-Series, which was also in development.

So the new MINI, while never pretending to create another technical revolution, still had the look and the Issigonis spirit of being as compact as possible. From the first drawings the key Mini cues were there. The 'floating' roofline above a straight waistline, the distinctive windscreen angle and a suggestion in the bonnet shutline of the defining MINI front-wing seam, round headlamps (albeit now racily raked back) and the classic 'smiley' grille shape were all evident, but far cleverer than just being clumsy copies of the original. Because what Frank Stephenson had done was genuinely to capture the Mini spirit.

While details changed during development, that fundamental Mini-ness didn't – to the credit of both BMW, who would ultimately have to sell it, and to the Rover team, charged with putting the concept into production. The wheels, for instance, were always huge compared with the original, but kept a classic sporty-Mini proportion. The Cooper look of contrasting body and roof colours was usually in evidence, too. And of course, the new MINI was transverse-engined and front-drive.

Under the skin it was to be considerably more complex than the original, with a different bias dictated by different times. At the same time, in driving dynamics as well as in looks, BMW were adamant for it to capture the essence of the Mini.

That meant class-leading handling and roadholding, with a degree of comfort that the original never came close to. It also meant ample performance, BMW build quality and (to some degree) equipment levels, plus meeting modern safety standards – the development target being a four-star rating in the NCAP system, which was still as good as it got for a MINI-sized package. (European NCAP is Europe's version of the New Car Assessment Programme – the stringent vehicle testing programme whose safety ratings are topped by the much sought after but rarely awarded five stars. American NCAP is the North American equivalent and of course the new MINI, with its worldwide sales plans, would have to be assessed under both.)

The outcome of the mechanical development was that the new MINI would use steel coil springs as a suspension medium rather than Rover's familiar Hydragas alternative. It would have strut front suspension and a version of BMW's Z-axle at the rear. And taking the official line that Rover's K-Series wouldn't fit, it would have a family of four-cylinder, 16-valve, 1.6-litre engines built in Brazil in a joint venture with Chrysler, who would use their own versions in the Neon saloon and PT Cruiser hatch.

Crucially, in defining the MINI's balance of quality feel with class-leading dynamics, it would have a super-stiff bodyshell on which to hang it all – a shell almost three times as stiff as a typical rival and stiff enough to make the original Mini look about as rigid as a piece of wet string. Which would, of course, have significant safety benefits, although the main safety issue was a familiar one – creating a big enough area of progressive deformation ahead of the passenger cell without compromising the short-bonneted proportions.

At the front that meant a massive amount of detail work in packaging the engine. It meant plenty of work to make the one-piece 'clamshell' bonnet with its integral headlamps light enough to open, stiff enough not to flutter its eyelashes and of a shape that they could actually build. At the back it meant a similar amount of effort in packaging the Z-axle multi-link suspension while still leaving acceptable (if not exactly generous) luggage room and space for two usable rear seats. All of which was complex enough for Rover's engineers to be more than justified in looking for the credit due in what they achieved.

Without labouring the point, BMW had certainly done front-wheel drive studies of their own, but they passed the responsibility for making the MINI work to Rover, who delivered. They had prototypes with real engines and real suspension on the road towards the end of 1997 – pretty well on cue for the planned production start at the end of 2000, for launch in summer 2001. That, naturally, pre-supposed not too much would go wrong in the testing programme – and, of course, a test programme wouldn't be one if things didn't go wrong – but they eventually got the MINI through on time. Once they had solved the admittedly quite major problem of having to shed some weight and add some power, the biggest problems were in making it buildable.

Another decision confirmed BMW's understanding of the heritage they'd taken on. It had clearly helped to have the Anglophile and badge-conscious Dr Pischetsrieder championing the MINI during its crucial development phase and it helped again when the decision was made about where to build it. The final commitment to building in the UK would be taken in April 2000, after Pischetsrieder had been ousted from Rover, but it basically confirmed what Pischetsrieder had said all along – that the MINI's heritage was British and that included being built in Britain. His successor, Joachim Milberg, stuck with that (even though BMW had divested itself of Rover before production was due to start) by retaining the plant already slated to build MINI.

As he said in October 2000, 'England remains an important production base for BMW. The MINI will be built at Oxford in our state-of-the-art plant.' Independently, Gert Hildebrand, who took over as head of the design studio in January 2001, referred to the Mini heritage as 'neo-European' and described the new MINI as being 'as clearly British as the new Beetle is clearly German'. And when the MINI was launched in 2001, BMW remained very definite about

describing it as 'A premium car – built in Britain'. In BMW-speak it was built in 'Plant Oxford', or as another generation had known it, Cowley, which had produced the first Mini Minor, in 1959.

The MINI Project Team relocated to the future plant in May 2000 and the pre-production build stage began, while in parallel, the installation of production facilities started in September 2000. In turning the ageing facilities into a suitably modern plant to build the new MINI to BMW standards, BMW invested more than £230 million specifically for this model, and another £80 million on upgrading shared paint-shop facilities. Volume production would start in April 2001, a year after the production decision was given to Oxford. Within a very short time 'Oxford' would employ around 4,500 people and the lines would be ramped up to building 500 MINIs a day. Given the car's reception at launch, it was soon obvious that that was barely enough.

One final, vital element had fallen into place during the development phase and that, of course, was the interior design – attributed by *Autocar* in 2001 to Rover's Wyn Thomas and Tony Hunter (who later moved to Land Rover). The interior is at least as show-stopping as the exterior, maybe even more so – it's full of big, bold features like the exposed aluminium-coloured dash, centre strut and door structures. Like the exterior it has classic Mini styling cues, notably in the centre instruments, the open shelf space underneath them, the row of toggle switches (brought up to modern safety requirements by clever shrouding) and even the stylised steering column stalks – although plans to put old-style

Making it. Robot lines at Plant Oxford create 21st-century build quality.

tell-tale lights on the ends were soon ditched.

The bottom line is that it again evokes the classic original while being absolutely modern, in fact radically imaginative. And as would become clear when it was finally ready to drive, it would have a quality feel way beyond the small-car norm.

While all this was happening, the MINI was gradually ramping up to its production launch, but with that still some way away, BMW were quite clever in drip-feeding the press and potential customers with further glimpses of the car.

The very first 'official' taster was offered in September 1997 when then R&D chief Wolfgang Reitzle, chairman Bernd Pischetsrieder and John Cooper unveiled a 'concept' car at the Frankfurt Motor Show. It was to all intents a full preview of the MINI, almost four years before launch.

As testing continued – and in a modern world that involved literally hundreds of prototypes – further info was drip-fed. In 1999 this included details of the engine, some transmission options, the Z-axle suspension, the interior and the rumoured price range. In September 1999 *Autocar* published a 'spy-shot' of a supposedly near-production spec car in Cooper S trim, taken by a reader when the car was displayed to a limited audience amid heavy security, at the classic Mini's 40th birthday party at Silverstone. In November they ran more 'world-first' scoop pictures, this time of the interior. In January 2000 there was confirmation that the brand would be taken back to America for the first time in decades. And then the problems began.

Not car problems but corporate ones again, as BMW decided to rid itself of Rover and the long and complicated process of who bought what from whom started to unfold, with MINI production plans unavoidably getting caught up in the middle. By January 2000 BMW were admitting that the production launch wouldn't happen until mid-2001. Through much of mid-2000 there were continuing doubts about the official reveal date as the sale of Rover dragged on, with competing bids from several consortiums. It was eventually resolved in May 2000 in favour of the 'Phoenix' group, but MINI, of course, remained firmly with BMW. And it was almost ready.

It made its public debut in 'production' form at the Paris Motor Show on 6 September, 2000. By April 2001 production had started in ever-increasing volume and the new MINI officially went on sale (in the UK first) on 7 July, 2001 in two versions – the 'entry-level' MINI One, at £10,300, and the MINI Cooper, at £11,600. These were very competitive prices. And in September 2001, when the car was launched in the rest of Europe in its next splash of markets, the prices were just as competitive. Which left only a launch in the USA, Japan and Australia early in 2002 to make the MINI, for the first time ever, a truly global product.

One sad aspect of the launch timing was that John Cooper never saw the new car on sale. The man who, after Issigonis, contributed more than anyone else towards the Mini legend, died on 24 December, 2000. He was 77, had grown up in a garage-owning family, studied as an engineeer and had famously pioneered single-seater racing cars with the engine behind the driver in the late 1940s – making Cooper the world's biggest

Plenty to smile about. Gert Hildebrand, who saw the MINI through its final stages to production.

manufacturer of single-seater racing cars. His Cooper Car Company won two Formula One constructors world championships, in 1959 and 1960, and created the Mini Cooper in 1961.

By the time John Cooper died, the various guardians of the Mini name had produced around a quarter of a million cars bearing the Cooper name. John Cooper changed the Mini from utility car to sporting icon and kick-started its success. And when Mini sales were flagging, it was the re-launch of the Cooper in 1990 that breathed new life into sales once again. It was Cooper, too, who created the fastest first-generation production Mini of all in the 1999 Cooper S Works. So when BMW planned the new MINI,

Cooper's name was linked with it from the start.

The first version of the new MINI most of us drove was the Cooper version and basically we loved it. The following is distilled from what I wrote after my own first test and it still holds true:

'The new MINI doesn't reinvent the small car as the original did, but its winning combination of generous dollops of classic Mini DNA, plus thoroughly modern technology, performance, safety and quality, has moved the game on a few squares. It was a long time coming and anyone who loved the old car probably waited with some trepidation, but in the end the new MINI has been quickly accepted as one of the best small-car packages around. In many areas as the best, full

The dramatic shapes and materials in this development interior largely survived into production models.

stop. It mixes massive personality with build and trim quality that rewrites the small-car rules, plus price and equipment levels to give many competitors nightmares and a ride and handling balance to bring a smile to the face of the most sceptical, most die-hard old-Mini enthusiast.

'All [One, Cooper and forthcoming 'range-topping, supercharged, seriously hot-hatch' Cooper S] have versions of a new four-cylinder, 16-valve, 1.6-litre engine built for BMW by Chrysler, with 90bhp in MINI One, 115bhp in MINI Cooper, and 163bhp in MINI Cooper S. In One that offers 115mph, 0–62mph in 10.9 seconds, and a combined fuel figure of 43.5mpg.

Cooper ups the stakes to 125mph, 9.2 seconds and a still useful 42.2mpg – Cooper S will add another dimension again.

'The Cooper is an impressive introduction to new generation Mini motoring. It's the sort of car that will be a must-have for any style-conscious buyer – and in that respect the new MINI has absolutely no baggage to cope with, because the old Mini never, ever lost its anti-style stylishness. The inside is terrific: brave, imaginative, kicking convention – happy and big-smile making while succeeding in being very practical. Not everybody will like it, especially the big central speedo and huge splashes of silver scaffolding,

The start of something big? Small car in the Big Apple – MINI in New York, tomorrow the world.

but come on, lighten up a bit, there's nothing wrong with being bold and different. Anyway, just have a look at the quality.

'This is where MINI starts to motor away from the opposition. It's built by BMW (in Britain) and BMW values scream out. Rear seat room is tight and the boot is verging on token but, as Issigonis said about the original, if it was any bigger it wouldn't be a MINI. The driving position is superb, the control layout, with its row of new-wave toggle switches in the middle and Buck Rogers stalks on the column, is delightful. It has loads of useful oddment spaces, and most striking of all is the incredible big-car feel. It has

exceptional trim quality (including the option of part or full leather) and feels solid as a rock – a world apart from some small-car rivals.

'Expectations for this car were spectacularly high, partly because BMW had talked it up so much, partly because the original Mini was such a legend for its unfeasible ability. In terms of agility, the new MINI isn't an old Mini.

'Kart-like, in the way the old Mini was, isn't feasible any more. But by 2001 standards MINI is in a class of its own for its broad reach of on-road talent. If it lacks one thing it is low down flexibility, but the 1.6, 16v is so willing further up the range (and sounds so much in tune with the car), gear ratios are so well chosen and the gearshift so superb, that you easily drive your way past it. In any case, the Cooper leaves any direct opposition for dead in headline performance and the S should settle the argument, full stop.

'But the clincher is the combination of grip, steering, brakes, handling and ride comfort. The MINI is everything BMW promised and that's some achievement.'

The Cooper S arrived early in 2002, with a supercharged version of the 1.6-litre engine and a big power increase. Many had waited with some trepidation, wondering whether the iconic badge could stand up in the 21st century as a seriously hot hatch. They needn't have worried – the new S proved to be as big a leap over 'ordinary' MINIs as the original S had been almost 30 years before. A bit more flamboyant, with bonnet scoop, side vents, bigger wheels, exposed filler cap, roof spoiler and twin exhausts, but a MINI still.

Extensive modifications meant the S would be reliable and acceptably economical, but its belt-driven supercharger gave it the only engine in its class to beat 100bhp per litre – 163bhp and 155lb per ft of torque, widely spread. So on the road, the new Cooper S was defined by ample power, great responses and huge flexibility – backed by a superb six-speed gearbox with close ratios and as quick and positive a shift as you'd find anywhere. With a power to weight ratio of around 140bhp per ton, that gave a maximum of 135mph with 0–62mph in 7.4 seconds and 50–75mph in just 6.7 seconds, which is very punchy indeed.

Other things had changed since the 1960s. The new S's standard equipment included ventilated front and solid rear disc brakes, ABS anti-lock, EBD (Electronic Brakeforce Distribution), CBC (Cornering Brake Control) and ASC+T (Automatic Stability Control with Traction control), or alternatively Dynamic Stability Control as an option – an electronic safety armoury even Issigonis would never have dreamt of. What he *would* have recognised was how the new S took Mini character and brought it up to date. Its dynamics remained razor sharp to a degree that made other small cars seem dull. With the stiffest suspension, biggest wheels and lowest profile tyres, it doesn't give a limousine ride but does deliver the most agile and exploitable car imaginable. The brakes are powerful, the steering, at only two-and-a-half turns between locks, is even quicker than on other MINIs and the S changes direction as quickly as you can flex your wrists. That's the Cooper S' real strength. Drive it as hard as you like, it will respond faithfully, tell you everything and let you be involved.

There was another bit of history for the new Cooper S. Even before it went on sale in Europe, it debuted in America – and anyone who might have thought that was a step too far was in for a surprise. Weeks before the official launch the author drove a new Cooper S around New York, through every kind of district – from the cash-drippingly chic to the ever-so-nearly scary – and stopped them dead in their tracks. They loved it. They crossed the street to talk about it. They pulled alongside in traffic to hoot their approval. Even style-obsessed Chelsea and Greenwich Villagers whooped. They couldn't get enough of

New MINI under the skin – a far cry from Issigonis' early Mini sketches on envelopes and menus.

it. And somehow, even in New York, the Cooper S looked completely at home. By American standards (even now 'normal'-sized European and Japanese cars are everywhere) the MINI is very small. Yet even in among the big yellow cabs and battleship-sized pick-ups and people carriers, it has such a giant personality that it doesn't *look* small. And, as we know, America loves larger than life characters.

Tom Purves, one-time boss of BMW UK and the man charged with the task of taking MINI to America, reckoned that although only around 10,000 original Minis had trickled into America in the car's heyday, the Mini wasn't as unknown as we might imagine, 'at least among a small but influential group of Americans who travelled in their youth, worked, lived, possibly even married abroad, who in some way were exposed to the Mini in the 1960s and 1970s in Europe. They never forgot it. I meet people regularly who remember the Mini because their wife or husband drove one, or they drove one themselves, maybe even raced or rallied one in Europe, and want to be a part of MINI today. They smile when they remember an extraordinary little car that went round corners like nothing else on earth, they remember the excitement, and they see the same things again in the new MINI.

'They see the looks recreating the classless personality of the original, then they drive it and think, "Wow! This is serious!" So, yes, that small group is very influential. The car itself might not have a US heritage, but it already has what you might call "bragging at the bar" rights. "I've got a new MINI" means "Did you know this was the most successful European small car? Do you know it won the Monte Carlo Rally? Do you know who drove them?"

'That whole association with pop stars and royalty and movie stars does the MINI no harm at all, even with people who never saw the old one in the flesh. America loves personalities, personality is America's class system. If a Mini was a car that Paul McCartney drove, if a Mini was something members of the royal family drove, or the Rolling Stones used, if a Mini was associated with Peter Sellers, that's all positive …

'So in many dealerships in America you'll see a wall of MINI heritage, showing the 1960s and Mary Quant and people like her with Minis. That's a valuable part of the mosaic that goes into launching the brand, but it isn't the bedrock of the brand. That's the concept of real motoring, of actually having fun behind the wheel – which is one thing the new MINI delivers in spades.'

And who would buy it in America? A week before the US launch, Tom Purves was pretty clear: 'One thing that's obvious from market research is that it's more about mind-set than age or an income group. One sales girl told me, "They're absolutely all ages. We had a 65-year-old lady BMW owner who traded her BMW for a MINI. Or a 20-year-old whose family had never

had anything to do with BMW but thought the MINI was the perfect car." It's very exciting, and it brings us a whole new bunch of customers.'

In America the ads read 'MINI. Let's motor!' Sales certainly did, from day one. Officially, the Cooper started from $16,300, the S at $19,300. Within days cars were advertised privately at large premiums as waiting lists grew. Soon the Cooper S was also available in Europe and the MINI was on sale virtually around the world – in effect for the first time in the badge's history. The awards had started to flow – 'car of the year' plaudits not only from magazines and organisations in Britain but around the world. In January 2003 the MINI Cooper was named North American Car of the Year at the Detroit International Auto Show – a real achievement for a British-built car.

Sales were already strong enough to make production capacity in Oxford the MINI's most serious worry. Mike Cooper, son of John Cooper, had continued the tradition of even more special after-market MINI performance with the 'Cooper Works' versions of the new car, and new MINIs had started a new racing career, in open classes as well as in a one model series, the John Cooper Challenge, dedicated to the man who made the Mini buzz.

BMW, too, insisted that MINI was no longer one car but now a full-blown brand. Other versions would follow, the expectation being the first would probably be a convertible variant – not to mention a second generation of this second generation, which would move the game on yet again. So as it headed for its 50th anniversary, the MINI had never looked stronger.

Stunt driver Russ Swift does amazing things with MINIs, journalist James May perfects 'not at all nervous' grin.

'We wanted the **first impression** when you walk up to the car to be "it could only be a **Mini**."'

Frank Stephenson (to **Autocar** magazine, 2001)

chapter twelve

When an icon is **reborn**, there's more than a passing chance that any **love affair** may be fleeting, in other words, that the novelty will soon **wear off**, but in that respect, too, the new MINI defied all stereotypes.

Success

MINI approaching fifty fast

Do ensure you have a real MINI before filling up... part of the MINI adventure ad campaign.

Until the global financial dramas of 2008 and 2009 moved the goalposts for everybody, the MINI's sales success was relentless and its popularity unwavering. But, like the Mini before it, the MINI never stood still for long.

It was always in the game plan, of course, that MINI would no longer be just a car, it would be a brand, and a brand with multiple facets. So it wasn't long before BMW started to work seriously on the variants that had been on the cards from the beginning – starting with a body configuration that had given the original Mini a challenge it never really solved very convincingly, in the form of the first new MINI Convertible.

But before outlining the cars, it's worth remembering the position BMW had happily achieved, working now with a huge degree of confidence, and with good reason. The new MINI was unequivocally a success; over launch weekend alone, more than 50,000 people had visited MINI dealerships. In May 2002, less than a year after launch, an electric blue Cooper S (one of more than 4000 ordered by UK customers even before the S went on sale) became the 100,000th MINI off the line. By the end of 2002, the MINI would be available in fifty markets worldwide, from giants like the UK, USA, Japan and Europe to minnows like Guadeloupe and Bahrain.

(Previous Page) 2009 John Cooper Works Convertible, probably going over fifty.

To meet demand, Plant Oxford was now working a seven-day week while the imminent arrival of the gap-filling diesel powered MINI in 2003 meant they'd probably need to build even more. This prompted plant managing director Dr Herbert Diess to announce an increase in production of around 15 to 20 per cent over the originally planned 100,000 cars a year, following a further £50 million worth of investment. And this wouldn't be the last time that Oxford would have to find ways of building ever more cars.

Like the Mini, too, the MINI was fast becoming a celebrity in its own right. To commemorate its first Christmas, a 50-foot Christmas tree made of twelve life-size fibreglass MINIs floated on the Thames for two weeks; as part of MINI's 2001 'guerrilla-marketing activities' thirteen more life-size MINIs were seen 'driving' up landmark buildings across UK cities; the first John Cooper Challenge attracted 25 entries to its inaugural season of hill climbs, sprints and races; and, in another bit of déjà vu, MINI customers started to personalise their cars with new roof décor options including St George and Union Jack flags, with more in the pipeline. Visibility was rarely an issue – in September 2002 the 'It's a MINI Adventure' road show covered 2500 miles, with 822 people getting behind the wheel of one MINI to produce, according to Guinness World Records, the 'World's Most Driven Car'.

Then, in May 2003, at the BMW AG shareholder meeting in Munich, Director of the Board Dr Panke revealed the next steps in MINI's future. 'With the MINI One D,' he announced, 'we are expanding the MINI model range in Europe. It is the first MINI ever with a diesel engine, and with this variant we will make MINI even more attractive for the European markets…' But that wasn't all: ending long speculation about an open-top variant, and responding to considerable customer pressure, he also announced that the family would soon be further extended by that MINI Cabriolet. 'The MINI brand,' he said, 'is an important pillar of our premium brand strategy and we are continuing with our investments. I can hereby confirm that we will be expanding the MINI product range by a four-seater cabrio, with the aim of gaining new customers in the open-top small car segment. The MINI Cabrio will become another highlight in the success story of the MINI brand…'

He was right. Previous year's sales of some 144,000 cars had exceeded expectations by about 40 per cent, and by March 2003 total sales had passed the 200,000 mark, led by the UK, US and German markets, in that order. With no signs of the novelty factor wearing off, the half-million milestone was reached in September 2004, with a Cooper S destined for the USA, wearing a commemorative plaque on its engine cover. BMW boasted that 500,000 MINIs end-to-end would stretch from Land's End to John O'Groats, and that with 50,000 possible permutations of options and accessories (from bonnet stripes to ICE systems), statistically, each of the half million built to date need only have nine others in the world exactly like it. The latest countries to join the network included South Korea, Argentina, Bulgaria and Venezuela – while the USA alone sold its 100,000th MINI in February 2005, fully two years ahead of forecast, and now had 80 dealers country-wide.

Just as Tom Purves had predicted before launch, the US market stretched from sea to shining sea. Led by New York, South Florida and California, America enthusiastically embraced MINI culture: in 2004 MINI drivers turned up from all over the USA to a Nevada MINI Owners Club event, and in 2005 more than 150 MINIs (including the author's) would descend on Las Vegas to drive in convoy through the city, over the Hoover Dam and deep into the Red Rock Canyon on the Club's annual 'MINI Vacation in Vegas'.

By the MINI's fifth birthday, in July 2006, more than 800,000 had been sold around the world, in over 70 markets, and there were eight models in the range – MINI One, MINI One D, MINI Cooper, MINI Cooper S, MINI One Convertible, MINI Cooper Convertible, MINI Cooper S Convertible and MINI Cooper S with John Cooper Works GP Kit. Celebrating the birthday, Plant Oxford's new boss Anton Heiss said 'it is not just the high quality of vehicles produced here but also the customer focus and production flexibility that have played such a major role in the car's success. Year-on-year we have produced record production figures. The £100 million investment programme currently underway will allow us to increase production flexibility and capacity further and meet growing worldwide demand'.

That still showed no sign of tailing off; 2005's record production of 200,119 cars was more than double the original prediction of 100,000 a year. MINI was now the third largest car manufacturer in the UK and a big contributor to the UK economy, with almost 80 per cent of the cars it was building being destined for export. MINI's worldwide tally

of awards had also comfortably exceeded one hundred. Yet MINI, in spite of its Bavarian patronage, remained resolutely British in terms of production, with Oxford as one side of the 'MINI triangle', supported now by the new BMW Plant Hams Hall near Birmingham (from where all future MINI petrol engines would come) and BMW Group Plant Swindon, in Wiltshire, which supplied body pressings and sub-assemblies.

The millionth MINI arrived in April 2007, headed for BMW's Mobile Tradition heritage centre. This Pepper White Cooper S sported a specially developed paint for its roof (Almond Green, accentuated by a 'million' graphic extending onto the bonnet) and a matching interior with seats, steering wheel and gearknob all in Almond Green leather.

So, in a little under six years and those million cars, the MINI had come a very long way, and the first big step had come two years into the story with the launch of that key power option that had never been available to the original Mini, but which was becoming increasingly important for optimising sales even in the small-car segments. And this really was a big departure – as the MINI finally discovered diesel.

In the heyday of the original Mini, diesel was not what it is today. Back then, heavy and noisy diesel engines were still far more at home in trucks, tractors and taxis, and the small diesel was a rare beast indeed. Any diesel small enough to fit into the snugly packaged original Mini would have been impossibly short on both power and manners, so it simply didn't happen, and at the time it was no big loss. But by the time the new MINI arrived, the

The millionth MINI, a second generation Cooper S, rolling off the production line at Oxford in April 2007.

latest generation of turbocharged diesels with common-rail injection and sophisticated emissions counter-measures were a completely different proposition. Now modern technology and modern metallurgy meant compact dimensions and relatively light weight were no longer the exclusive domain of the spark ignition engine, so enjoying diesel economy no longer meant sacrificing acceptable power and refinement. Finally, diesel was a viable alternative to petrol even in a car as diminutive as the MINI.

As Panke revealed, it arrived in May 2003, in the MINI One D. Projected to sell between 10,000 and 20,000 cars a year, it was perfectly positioned to be another MINI success story. America didn't understand it yet, but diesel for the family car was already widely accepted across Europe, and its popularity was growing fast in the UK; official figures just before the One D's arrival showed that UK diesel sales had increased for 30 consecutive months since late 2000, and were expected to account for one third of all new cars in 2003.

So the MINI's fourth power option (alongside the One, Cooper and Cooper S) was a lightweight, all-aluminium, turbocharged and intercooled, common-rail direct-injection four-cylinder 1.4-litre

D Day, the MINI One D at launch in 2003.

diesel engine. It was developed in cooperation with Toyota and specifically tailored for the MINI's compact engine bay. And, crucially, it gave the kind of performance any MINI owner would demand, even with diesel in the tank.

In typical diesel fashion, its character was more about widely spread flexibility than maximum power, combining a relatively modest 75bhp with a thumping 180Nm of torque at just 2000rpm. That made it equally suited to stop-start city driving or rapid progress across country, with a top speed of 103mph, 0–62mph in 13.5 seconds, but more tellingly, the deep-down grunt to go from 50 to 75mph in fourth gear in only 11.9 seconds. Making

the most of the delivery, it used its own version of the Cooper S's six-speed gearbox, with a long sixth gear to keep revs low and economy high at cruising speeds. Together, that meant 58.9mpg on the EU combined cycle, corresponding to CO_2 emissions of just 129g/km – making the MINI One D the most fuel-efficient car in the whole BMW Group.

It was refined, too, as the best new generation diesels are, and nothing about it required any real compromise in the MINI's sporty dynamics. To tame its low-speed torque on slippery surfaces, it adopted ASC+T (Automatic Stability Control+Traction) alongside other elements of the usual MINI safety armoury, such as four airbags, all disc brakes, ABS, EBD (Electronic Brakeforce Distribution), and CBC (Cornering Brake Control) all as standard, helping the MINI One D to four stars in the Euro NCAP safety ratings.

Externally, it was much like any other MINI, save for the badges, a revised air-intake layout, concealed tailpipe, and Cooper S sills. At the Frankfurt Motor Show in September, the MINI One D sat alongside its siblings: the 'entry level' MINI One, with 1.6-litre 16-valve four-cylinder engine, 90bhp, a top speed of 112mph, and 0–62 mph in 10.9 seconds; the MINI Cooper, with 115bhp, delivering 62mph in 9.2 seconds with a top speed of 124mph; and the supercharged, 163bhp, 135mph, 7.4 seconds-to-62mph Cooper S, distinguished by Sports PLUS suspension, air-scoop bonnet, body colour bumpers, rear spoiler, distinctive sills, side vents with the 'S' logo, twin chromed tailpipes and 16-inch alloy wheels.

Or if none of that was enough, Frankfurt 2003 offered one more option – the MINI Cooper S with official 'aftermarket' John Cooper Works tuning kit, offering a full 200bhp at a free-revving 6950rpm, a maximum of 140mph, bespoke 18-inch wheels, and sports seats.

What came next broadened the choice again, as the MINI finally lost its head – delivering Dr Panke's carrot of open-topped MINI motoring as promised, when the MINI Convertible made its world debut at the Geneva Show in March 2004.

They called it a full four-seater, a genuine MINI whether the roof was up or down. And in either configuration it looked far neater than the original Mini ever did with its top chopped off. A simple chrome strip around the lower glass line defined a softly rising waistline, and while the folded soft-top was still too big to hide, proportionally it was much less of a problem than it had been on the much smaller old car. The question of rollover protection was answered quite neatly too, with a simple pair of polished aluminium hoops behind the rear backrest, and strong beams concealed in the windscreen A-pillars. So, a much tidier looking chop than before and the MINI audience loved it.

It came to market with the choice of MINI One or MINI Cooper mechanicals, and the promise of a drop-top Cooper S to follow. The fabric roof offered three colours the unique feature of an integral sliding panel (in effect a sunroof) that opened over the front seats without having to open the whole roof – a serious bit of sophistication on such a small car. The full, powered soft-top could be raised or lowered in just fifteen seconds at the touch of a button, stowing in an acceptably neat way over the rear parcel shelf area, without the need for a separate cover. And while rear passenger and boot space were snug as ever, the Convertible did reprise one famous feature of the oldest Minis, with a bottom-hinged boot lid that folded down, and, tethered by two steel cables, could carry up to 176 lb. Actually, putting the roof down reduced the 165-litre boot capacity to just 120 litres, but they did offer 'Easy Load' for through-loading longer items, and you could also drop the rear seats completely, if you wanted to carry luggage rather than passengers.

BMW had done a fine job of replacing the stiffness that losing the roof inevitably imposes (not to mention keeping safety up to the highest standards), so the open-top MINI again didn't ride

MINI convertible at the push of a button.

or handle much differently to any other. The extra 100kg or so of shell reinforcement and roof mechanism obviously blunted performance a little, but not so much as to be a huge problem. You could also specify the Convertible with virtually any options available on any other MINI, and a few of its own, so, of course, it was another instant winner, in effect doubling the MINI choices at a stroke.

From September 2005 the MINI One D became an even more tempting alternative to gasoline. Revised management, new injectors and exhaust gas re-circulation with a large-capacity catalytic converter improved peak power by almost 20 per cent. That additional 13bhp helped trim

almost two seconds from 0–62mph, and raised top speed to 109mph. The diesel strong point of big flexibility was also further improved, with peak torque up by 10Nm to 190Nm, now spread all the way from 1800 to 3000rpm. Even better, the stronger performance created no penalty in economy, and a combined consumption exactly as before of 58.9mpg still gave the revised MINI One D a potential range of 600 miles on a single tank, while being fully compliant with the latest EU4 emission standards.

In ways that were barely an issue in the previous generation of Minis, huge efforts were made to ensure that the production process was as

Clubman Concept at the Tokyo Motor Show , October 2005. Anyone fancy a picnic?

environmentally responsible as possible. Between 2002 and the millionth MINI in 2007, continuous focus on more efficient use of natural resources saw Plant Oxford's energy consumption and CO_2 emissions both reduced by 20 per cent, while water consumption dropped by more than 30 per cent for each car built, and more than 25 different waste materials from production were now recycled.

Some fine old Mini traditions were being recycled too, including the massive get-together. In October 2005, 6000 fans from more than 40 countries attended the first international MINI United festival in Italy – mostly in their own cars as nearly 2000 new MINIs and classic Minis crowded

the Santa Monica racetrack in Misano. More than 250 made the 1000-mile journey from the UK, joining owners from Thailand, Japan, Australia and all over Europe, but the award for the longest drive of all went to Dimitri Kotov from Moscow who drove 2200 miles to be at MINI United. Just like in the old days, the festival combined off-piste entertainment with on-track opportunities, both competitive and just for the fun of it.

Pitting the fastest drivers from various national MINI Challenge Series against each other produced an inaugural 'MINI Challenge world champion' in Maxime Martin from Belgium, who beat drivers from ten countries including the UK,

Clubman at launch in 2007, showing just how much of the concept survived through to production.

USA, Germany, Sweden, Austria, Finland and Bahrain. The final race of the weekend, with ex-F1 drivers, Touring Car champions and Monte Carlo winners in identical 210bhp John Cooper Works MINI Cooper Ss, was won by FIA World Touring Car Champion Alessandro Zanardi.

MINIs, like Minis, enjoyed some long-distance adventures. In April 2006, three Cooper Ss reached Plant Oxford after a 49-day, 8000-mile run from South Africa, crossing ten more countries. The cars were essentially standard apart from taller ground clearance, heavy-duty dampers, all-terrain tyres on steel rims, and South African flag paintwork. From Johannesburg in March they went through Botswana, Zambia, Tanzania, Kenya, Ethiopia, Sudan and Egypt, carrying pretty well all the spares, sleeping equipment and supplies they

needed – where the rear seats and interior cladding used to be. Out of Africa they headed to the UK via Italy and France, and not one suffered a single mechanical breakdown.

Had they waited until late 2007 they could have carried rather more equipment, as the third body variant came to market, in the form of the MINI Clubman – the rebirth of the Mini estate car, or Traveller as it was once known, and a variant that had sold more than 400,000 examples between 1960 and 1982.

Like the diesel and the cabriolet, the Clubman's coming was an open secret, and this time there had been plenty of clues as to what to expect, starting at the Frankfurt Show in September 2005. Exactly 45 years after the launch of the original Mini Traveller in 1960, the MINI Concept Frankfurt presented 'a design study re-interpreting the philosophy of the little Traveller from Great Britain through a new concept of "Travelling in Style" befitting the beginning of the 21st century'.

Conceived under Design Director (and true Mini-phile) Gert Hildebrand, it stole the Show. Like the hatch, it evoked an iconic shape, while bringing both look and content right into the present, its lack of B-pillars giving an almost coupé-like sportiness. But the stunning, pale silver Concept was far cleverer than simple pastiche. While dominated by details like big, arch-filling wheels, strong shoulder line and carbonfibre-framed roof, the aim was practicality – to make loading and access as easy as possible. Huge front doors swung out and forwards in one movement; the rear sliding windows opened electrically; and the double rear door was vertically split just like the original, but each half opened on complex parallelogram hinges in the minimum of space. Its lid flush with the luggage compartment floor, the sunken 'Cargobox' provided hidden storage that lifted out for easy access, while its cover could be folded out as a loading platform for heavier items, or lifted to form a partition between passenger and luggage areas. The rear section of the roof also slid forwards, again for easy loading.

The 'Floating Elements' interior was pretty dramatic, too, with 'suspended' seats and 'hovering' dashboard – but showy as it was, you knew that, given the response the Concept received, it could only be a matter of time before the arrival of the more restrained real thing.

BMW showed another version of the Concept at the Tokyo Show in October 2005, featuring 'British' twists – a roof system that stored a picnic table and chairs, and a side-window mounting Cargobox table. Other details to wow the Anglophile Japanese included Union Jack motifs on bonnet and indicators. Then, at the Detroit Show in January 2006 (where they showed a third Concept, featuring a winter sports theme and the colours of the Stars and Stripes), they confirmed that the estate would evolve into a production model, the third MINI body configuration. At Geneva in March 2007 they announced it would be called the Clubman and would be on sale before the end of the year.

But before all that, in November 2006, the 'second generation' MINI went on sale, after previewing at the Paris Show. First up were the new MINI Cooper and MINI Cooper S. Far more than a facelift, this was a largely new car, echoing ever more demanding safety and emissions requirements, and driven by the extraordinary success of the first generation. Building more than twice the predicted numbers had aged the tooling quicker than planned, and vital upgrading of the Oxford production facilities (where investment between 2000 and 2007 now totalled £380 million) offered an unmissable opportunity to accelerate changes to the car into the same investment cycle. Reaction to those early Concept showings also meant pressure was growing to bring the Clubman's production launch forwards – and that car had to be based on the new platform, as it was when it duly appeared in March 2007.

Sensibly, though, for the new generation hatches, Hildebrand and his design team 'deemed evolution preferable to revolution', reckoning the best way ahead for MINI was to evolve in much the same way as the Porsche 911, not changing for the sake of change. Noting that the MINI had so far had only six years of exposure where Mini had 42, Hildebrand said that 'part of the success of the MINI is to do with the fact that it didn't change. Because it is functionally designed, there is no reason to change it. From the beginning we did only one model of something else. Logical evolution is the only way. And we wanted to protect the values of the previous version'. Fifty years on, this was thinking worthy of Issigonis himself.

So the new hatch's looks remained instantly recognisable, but every panel was different. There were changes inside, too, and a new family of engines with lower consumption and significantly reduced emissions. The nose was re-proportioned both to accommodate the new engines and fulfil future safety requirements, especially on pedestrian impact. In fact the new MINI was around 2½ inches longer, with reshaped grille and front bumper; the shoulder line was a little higher, to emphasise the sporty stance; and to simplify production and reduce costs the headlights became part of the main body rather than being built as before into a complex and expensive clamshell bonnet. But none of it remotely changed the key look.

Inside, far from losing the quirkiness, they went even more adventurous, and even more up-market – in their words, 'an all-new interior that aims to mix MINI's unique style with improved quality and greater comfort'. The signature central speedo was bigger than ever and included ICE controls in its bottom half, while both detail quality and content had moved even further up-market. There was new

soft, tone-adjustable lighting, an improved sat-nav system, and improved audio and communication interfaces – including iPod and Bluetooth connectivity that could only make you smile if you thought back to an original Mini's optional radio.

They even claimed more usable interior space, both front and rear, but these gains were strictly limited. The biggest improvement was actually a far better front-seat folding mechanism, replacing one of the original MINI's flakiest features.

Totally new BMW-built four-cylinder 1.6-litre petrol engines from Hams Hall were another big improvement, featuring far more technical sophistication than the rather dull first-generation units built in partnership with Chrysler in Brazil. The 1.6-litre naturally-aspirated MINI Cooper engine introduced fully variable valve control (based on BMW's unique VALVETRONIC system) to adjust inlet valve-lift and opening times within fractions of a second, in order to balance mid-range flexibility with top-end power and economy.

The new twin-cam 16-valve Cooper S engine used direct injection and a twin-scroll turbocharger with intercooler to deliver 173bhp and 177lb ft of torque – with short bursts of 'overboost' taking that to 192lb ft. The claimed figures were 140mph and 0–62mph in 7.1 seconds, and while the turbocharged engine wasn't quite as dramatic as the old supercharged one, it was far more civilised and significantly more economical. In a market conscious of both running costs and emissions-related tax implications, official consumption had improved from 32.8 to 40.9mpg while CO_2 emissions had plummeted from 207 to a much more acceptable 164g/km. Even the six-speed

MINI Cooper S with John Cooper Works Tuning Kit taking a break in Dubai, 2003.

gearshift was nicer, further underlining the changed character of the car as more refined and up-market.

As for ride and handling, they had, if anything, made the already brilliant MINI even better, with revised suspension underpinned by an even stiffer shell – which allowed for a more comfortable ride but without compromising the trademark agility and feel. There was enough power going to the front wheels, of course, to make them scrabble occasionally if pushed hard, but the electro-hydraulic power steering was terrific, the balance easily adjusted by more or less throttle, and an impressively flat cornering stance. In short, it was an even better MINI.

The Clubman duly arrived at Geneva 2007, looking commendably like the Concepts and criticised only for a door layout better suited to left- rather than right-hand-drive markets. Alongside it, BMW revealed a revised MINI One and highly economical MINI Cooper D (replacing the D), both in the new shape. The new entry-level One introduced a 95hp 1.4-litre petrol engine, derived from the 1.6-litre all-aluminium unit in the current Cooper, with VALVETRONIC-based variable valve control. Its 5bhp power increase and 140Nm of torque offered 0–62mph in 10.9 seconds and a maximum of 115mph, with average consumption of 49.6 mpg – a valuable gain of 15 per cent over its predecessor.

Combining Cooper and D badges for the first time showed that diesel was going sporty, too, with improved performance and economy from an all-new 1.6-litre 110bhp turbodiesel. With variable turbine geometry and second-generation common rail technology it offered 177lb ft of torque, with 'overboost' giving an additional 15lb ft in short bursts – figures identical to those for the new, petrol-powered Cooper S. That promised 121mph and sub-10 seconds to 62mph, but the Cooper D was also the most fuel-efficient and cleanest MINI to date – improving even on the One D's combined 58.9mpg, with no less than 64.2mpg.

Both One and Cooper D had six-speed manual gearboxes as standard, the new One with the option of a six-speed Steptronic automatic with sequential paddle shift and 'Sports Button' option for shorter shift times and faster throttle response. Both used the suspension set-up introduced on the new Cooper and Cooper S, and the Cooper D was readily recognisable by a pronounced 'power dome' on its bonnet.

There were other variants at both ends of the spectrum. In summer 2006 the limited edition MINI Cooper S with John Cooper Works GP Kit sold out as soon as it was announced. This was hardly surprising. The 218bhp two-seater MINI GP, sitting on spectacular 18-inch alloy wheels, weighed some 40kg less than a standard Cooper S and reached 62mph in under 6.5 seconds, with a top speed of 146mph. But if you missed one, summer 2008 brought the first John Cooper Works models to be built on the production line rather than aftermarket. This had a GP-like performance, but this time with four seats. Headline figures were 6.5 seconds and 148mph from 211bhp and up to 207lb ft of torque on overboost. And it sounded wonderful.

At the other end of the scale, 2008 saw a MINI with almost no sound at all – the MINI E, a 240bhp two-seat electric-only MINI, in a 500-off production run for lease-only in selected US cities. With a 150-mile range, plug-in charging, a 95mph top speed, 8.5 seconds to 62mph, and zero emissions, it was a test bed for a possible future option.

But the present remained more conventional. With the half century approaching, the Convertible moved onto the new platform in March 2009, initially as Cooper and Cooper S, with the One due later. Again, the changes weren't easy to spot, except for a new one-piece rollover hoop which was normally concealed and only popped up if needed – a neater layout which also improved rear visibility with the roof down. As ever, body stiffening added weight, but the new cabrio was still lighter than the old one, and few would be disappointed by the drop-top Cooper S's 138mph potential and 7.4 seconds to 62mph.

The final twist on the MINI's way to fifty, though, was not of its own making. When the motor industry hit the skids in the global financial meltdown of 2008 and 2009, even MINI felt the shockwaves, with unavoidable production cutbacks and job losses. But it was a crisis in Suez that had created the Mini in the 1950s, and in their first half century Mini and MINI had survived, even thrived, through many other such crises. The MINI, face it, had even weathered the abysmal 2002 remake of *The Italian Job*. So one more drama was probably just another MINI Adventure – for what's still one of the greatest cars in motoring history.

Another MINI adventure survived, The Italian Job *the remake.*

' MINI's big **potential** is that it was designed to be **timeless** '

Gert Hildebrand (to **Pool** magazine)

You were only supposed to blow the bloody doors off. Minis on the roof, Alfa in pursuit. The Italian Job *(the original). The End.*

photographs

Advertising Archives p27, 85
Advertising Archives/BMIHT p21
BMW Great Britain p162, 167, 169, 175, 177, 179, 180, 183, 185, 186, 187, 189, 191, 193, 194, 197,198, 200, 201, 202, 205, 207
British Motor Industry Heritage Trust p161, 163, 164, 166, 170, 172
Broadspeed Engineering Ltd p6, 7, 60, 63, 113
Neill Bruce p18, 29 (both), 30, 34, 37, 74, 77, 87, 106, 119, 120, 122, 125, 152, 153
John Cooper p100
Hulton Getty p17, 45, 57, 65, 70, 78, 140
Hulton Getty/Derek Berwin p10 Hulton Getty/Cairns p59 Hulton Getty/Ron Case p151 Hulton Getty/Dumont p140 (bottom) Hulton Getty/John Downing p55 Hulton Getty/Douglas Miller p52
Hulton Getty/J. Wilds p61, 147
National Motor Museum p9, 11, 23, 43, 51, 93, 97, 98, 126, 127
Opie Collection p15, 66, 72
Pictorial Press p56, 81
Pictorial Press/K. Renton p133, 154, 156, 157, 159
Quadrant Picture Library p47, 53, 69, 76, 89,139, 142, 148
Quadrant Picture Library/C. Kent p95
Rex Features p75
Peter Roberts Collection, The /Neill Bruce p12, 24, 33, 39, 40, 83, 86, 88,103, 104 (both), 105, 107, 108, 109 (bottom), 111, 114, 117, 129, 131, 135, 145, 155, 158
Ronald Grant Archive p58, 192
Rover Group/BMIHT/Beaulieu p48, 86 (top), 90, 109 (top), 130, 137